PRAISE FOR GEORGE ZIMMER

"Over the decades, I've had to deal with George Zimmer on his sartorial expertise. I've always been a fan of his, and this book explains why."

—**Willie Brown**, former mayor of San Francisco

"George Zimmer is one of the finest political historians that I know. He is a courageous stalwart of progressive ideals and democracy. This book is a great read."

—**Jim Gonzalez**, former San Francisco supervisor

"Since my first encounter with George Zimmer in a private, closed-door meeting with Mikhail Gorbachev at the State of the World Forum back in 1999, I have valued George as a special counsel and my personal ethical guide for all my work in the disparate fields. He is a genuine American treasure and a revolutionary visionary, with a famous voice that can now be turned to saving us from ourselves—if we are ready to listen again. I guarantee it!"

—**Daniel Sheehan**, general counsel to the United States Jesuit Order's National Office of Social Ministry in Washington, DC, and founder of the Christic Institute and the Romero Institute

"From the moment I met George Zimmer I knew we were in the presence of a very great man. George came to speak to the children of Northern Light School as one of our Impossible Is Nothing speakers. He shared with them his secret to persevering throughout his many years of overcoming tremendous obstacles, making history, and leaving his profound mark on others and the business world as founder and head of one of the most prominent and successful companies throughout this country. As he spoke, I listened with great admiration to his profound words characterized by compassion, wisdom, dedication, commitment, and unconditional love."

—**Michelle Lewis**, founder and executive director of Northern Light School

"I left a career at the Men's Wearhouse to go back to work for George Zimmer. He is a great boss—and his book is pretty good too."

—**Jason Jackson**, president of Generation Tux

"*I Guarantee It* shows the rewards of determination, hard work, believe in yourself, and vision."

—**Joel Parrot**, president and CEO of the Oakland Zoo

"George Zimmer is one of my dearest friends who long ago made a commitment to support the things that mattered most to the city of Oakland. His incredible commitment to the Oakland Zoo, and to the children of Northern Light School, has given me such hope for the future of this beautiful city."

—**Cornell C. Maier**, World War II veteran, retired chairman and CEO of Kaiser Aluminum

"George Zimmer has always been the first to step up to the plate. He has always been my ace, my number one closer for getting the job done. George is my number one MVP in my Hall of Fame. I guarantee that!"

—**Vida Blue**, retired Major League Baseball player and recipient of the Cy Young Award, 1971

"An unconventional, charismatic, enormously successful business leader, George Zimmer shows how to help people become better than they ever thought they could and how business can transform society for good."

—**Jeffrey Pfeffer**, professor of organizational behavior at Stanford's Graduate School of Business and author of *The Human Equation*

You're going to like the way ~~you look~~: *this reads.*

I Guarantee It

The Untold Story
Behind the Founder of
Men's Wearhouse

George Zimmer

BEYOND WORDS
Portland, Oregon

BEYOND WORDS

1750 S.W. Skyline Blvd., Suite 20
Portland, Oregon 97221-2543
503-531-8700 / 503-531-8773 fax
www.beyondword.com

First Beyond Words hardcover edition September 2021

BEYOND WORDS PUBLISHING is an imprint of Simon & Schuster Inc., and the Beyond Words logo is a registered trademark of Beyond Words Publishing, Inc.

For information about special discounts for bulk purchases, please contact Beyond Words Special Sales at 503-531-8700 or specialsales@beyondword.com.

Managing Editor: Lindsay S. Easterbrooks-Brown
Copyeditor: Ashley Van Winkle
Proofreader: Madison Schultz
Design: Devon Smith
Composition: William H. Brunson Typography Services

Manufactured in Canada

10 9 8 7 6 5 4 3 2 1

Library of Congress Cataloging-in-Publication Data

Names: Zimmer, George CEO, author.
Title: I guarantee it : the untold story behind the founder of men's
    wearhouse / George Zimmer.
Description: Portland, Oregon : Beyond Words, [2021]
Identifiers: LCCN 2021020362 (print) | LCCN 2021020363 (ebook) |
ISBN 9781582708416 (hardcover) | ISBN 9781582708430 (ebook)
Subjects: LCSH: Zimmer, George CEO. | Men's clothing industry. | Men's
    Wearhouse (Firm)—Biography.
Classification: LCC HD9940.A2 Z56 2021 (print) | LCC HD9940.A2 (ebook) |
    DDC 687.0811—dc23
LC record available at https://lccn.loc.gov/2021020362
LC ebook record available at https://lccn.loc.gov/2021020363

The corporate mission of Beyond Words Publishing, Inc.: *Inspire to Integrity*

Contents

Introduction   vii

1. Fortunate Son   1

2. Come Together   17

3. Transitions   35

4. The Adult Lemonade Stand   51

5. "I Guarantee It!"   69

6. Going Public   89

7. Paradigm Shifts   103

8. Pot Luck   117

9. The Price of Betrayal   129

10. Generation Next   153

Epilogue   165

Acknowledgments   173

Photographs   175

Appendix   193

Introduction

In the days and months after I got fired from the company that I started, all I could think and feel was . . . why?

Emotionally, spiritually, and psychologically, I'd been shattered.

I'd been married and divorced twice. I had four kids, including one who died. I'd had an abdominal aortic aneurysm, known as a "Triple A," and, more recently, emergency open heart surgery. What was I doing wrong? Turns out, not all that much.

Forty years earlier, I had launched the Men's Wearhouse with the faith of an idealist who believed that if you treated everybody with fairness, dignity, trust, and respect, then everybody would prosper. From the very beginning in our fun, frantic early years when it wasn't at all certain that we would survive, I held firmly to the belief that our future depended on the relationships we built with our employees, customers, suppliers, and neighbors. I held to that belief to the very end—a belief that allowed me to see what would become our success.

With a little help from my family and a beloved frat brother from college, I built the Men's Wearhouse from the ground up. We began our operation in a single store in a far-flung Houston strip mall, where we kept our receipts in a cigar box and didn't take checks or credit cards. By the time my hand-chosen chief executive officer and board of directors stabbed me in the back in the middle of 2013, the Men's Wearhouse had grown from that single location to more than 1,100 stores in the United States and Canada. We were doing $2.5 billion a year in sales. We were worth a conservative $1.4 billion.

Seven years later, the new company created by the people who threw me out had gone bankrupt, and the multibillion empire of the Men's Wearhouse had turned into dust.

This is a story of its rise and fall, from the heart of its creator, who saw the opportunity for success and had achieved it with his own hard work, the love and financial support of his family, and the help of a lifetime of friends he met along the way.

Millions of people knew us—knew me—by our slogan: "You're going to like the way you look. I guarantee it."

I grew up in the rich and leafy New York City suburb of Scarsdale, a son of privilege, although my father and mother both had to overcome major challenges: he was a World War II navigator who survived a Nazi prisoner-of-war camp after Hitler's artillery shot down his B-24 bomber over Austria during World War II, and she was an adopted orphan whose biological mother fled the Stalinist pogroms of the early Soviet era.

I jumped into the sixties with my eyes wide open when I went away to college. At Washington University in St. Louis, where I resisted the Vietnam War and took up a lifetime appreciation of smoking marijuana, I got my degree in economics and set off on a road of self-discovery, toward becoming a man.

My father, who worked in the apparel industry, introduced me to the business and put me to work as a traveling salesman. When I got cheated by an unscrupulous department store buyer, I decided to start my own men's clothing company to show the world how to do it right. We named it the Men's Wearhouse, and we built it into a strong local chain in southeast Texas before we found out that an honest merchant with strong television advertising could make the company a national brand. We competed hard and swamped our rivals, both large and small, and we went public, and became a darling of Wall Street.

If I'd learned anything over the decades, with the success and growth of the Men's Wearhouse, it was that most men quiver at the thought of having to buy their own clothes. I'd seen thousands of them walk into our stores in a nervous sweat. And I'd seen just as many walk out relieved and happy, with tailored, brand-name wardrobes that they could afford, that felt right, that would be appreciated by the people in their lives, and didn't take too long to buy.

Make no mistake: in serving our customers, nobody got more joy out of the experience than I did. I traveled the world, and I got to know our country—store by store and city by city. I had the honor of meeting two presidents, Bill Clinton and Barack Obama. I got high with Baba Ram Dass. I bought a house in Hawaii and got to know and become friends with rock stars, athletes, and some of the most dynamic innovators in a generation of American business, like John Mackey of Whole Earth Foods and Marc Benioff of Salesforce.

From the beginning of our experiment with the Men's Wearhouse, my partners and I sought to create a company known for its culture of heart as well as its smarts. We invested millions of dollars in our people, in training, in pay, in benefits—and in partying. We valued our employees' personal happiness, knowing that it translated into greater productivity and a higher level of service to the customer. We hired people who brought joy to their work and who lived their lives with a sense of fun, and oh, how we sought to stoke it. Maybe that's why *Fortune* magazine listed us among the top 100 companies in the country to work for, year after year after year.

The whole time I led the Men's Wearhouse, I'd never even heard the term "stakeholder capitalism." All we did was practice it, off a mission statement that aimed to nurture the creativity of our workforce and "strive toward becoming self-actualized people"—a tip of my philosophical hat to the top of the pyramid of humanist psychologist Abraham Maslow's "hierarchy of needs." Roughly defined, stakeholder capitalism means that all business decisions should take into account the interests of all stakeholder groups—workers, suppliers, the wider community, the environment—as well as the people who invest in the company. Stakeholder capitalism has become an international force in the last decade, with some of the biggest companies in the world now claiming to adhere to its principles. It represents a paradigm shift from an old model of capitalism, where the only thing a business needed to worry about was maximizing the wealth of its shareholders.

On top of all this, I nurtured some hobbies—ones that fed right back into the values of the Men's Wearhouse. I deepened my understanding of the need for progressive capitalism through the World Business Academy, a Santa Barbara think tank. I supported scientific breakthroughs with an infusion of mysticism as a board member of the Institute of Noetic Sciences in Petaluma, California. I became a major funder of the successful medicinal marijuana campaign in California that has since changed the perception of pot—and made it legal to obtain marijuana in one fashion or another in forty-nine states.

And then, everything changed.

Like any rational man in his mid-sixties who built a successful business and who wanted to ratchet down his managerial duties, I had game-planned my retreat from the Men's Wearhouse: an exit on my own terms. As far back as 2001, I knew I had to start thinking about picking a new CEO to replace me. My timetable toward transition gained urgency in 2002 when I learned that I had an abdominal aortic aneurysm that required surgery. A surgical rush job extracted me from immediate danger, but mortality can get your attention.

Knowing I wouldn't be in charge forever, I looked around to find the company's future leaders. I picked a former tie buyer who ably worked his way up in the company to replace me as chief executive officer, while I stayed on as executive chairman of the board. From the time the Men's Wearhouse went public in 1992, I hand-picked a team of talented businessmen and creative thinkers to serve as directors. Many of you have probably heard of one of them—Deepak Chopra, the writer who mines the meeting ground between science and spirit. I met and liked Deepak and asked him to join our board, along with several other similarly thoughtful people whom I had met during my explorations over the decades into my assorted spiritual, philosophical, and financial curiosities.

In the end, they all wanted me gone. The guy who had the vision for the company was taken out by a collection of executives and board members that he had put in place in the company to begin with, people with whom he shared deep philosophical and spiritual beliefs. How did this happen?

There were some issues between me and the executives, for example my resistance to the amount of money some of them wanted to pay themselves. There were a couple of significant but not deal-breaking business disagreements. And there was one very significant departure of thinking in which I wanted to take the company private and they didn't.

I think that all of those reasons paled, however, compared to our different levels of commitment to our founding ideals. I think my push to keep the Men's Wearhouse true to its mission ran headlong into their greed, which led to their betrayal not so much of me, but of the progressive nature of a company that used to be a model of stakeholder capitalism.

Really, what choice did our executive team and our board of directors have? They had to fire me. I'd gone rogue, an unconscious but lifetime devotee of the way of doing business that takes everybody into consideration, not just the investor class.

So they fired me. And it made me angry. It made me bitter. It made me look for revenge, before I came to the realization that I could not continue in this world with a heart filled with hate and a soul that required retribution. I realized that if I was to achieve my own self-actualization, I would somehow have to reject my own animosity, my own growing sickness of soul, as well as my ego.

Over the years, I did manage to put the anger to rest, and as I did, I came into a new feeling. I returned to the essence of myself, who and what I am—a businessman. An entrepreneur.

I'm a competitor who wants to build the best business possible and take it to the top of his market.

I'm a hippie—still. Even in the business world, I compete with that spirit, infusing love into everything I do.

I'm a progressive, a liberal, a capitalist of the stakeholder variety.

I'm a CEO, a business leader who always has his eye on the future, for new ways of doing things.

I'm a reader, a sports fan, a thinker, and a connoisseur of marijuana, which I smoke regularly, and which helps shape a world perspective that I formulate daily while sitting at the end of my couch in the hills of Oakland, California, between puffs, between cable-television news shows, between innings of A's games, between newspaper and magazine articles and the books on history, politics, and economics that line my shelves.

When I'm sitting around with no particular place to go, I run numbers through my head. I scratch out ideas on notebook paper. I see problems and my mind bounces toward business solutions. I'm enthralled by markets. I try to account for their shortcomings. I try to envision manners in which businesses can provide for society as a whole.

In my search for ways to create sustainable long-term value and be true to my merchant nature, I recently started up a new business. I call it Generation Tux, and my formal-wear rental business has since taken off. You may have seen—I'm back on TV, selling it.

My life that had become derailed in self-pity and self-regard has been placed back on track, with revitalized purpose of building this company on the vision of a sustainable stakeholder capitalism.

A shattered spirit had been restored.

⊸ 1 ⊢

Fortunate Son

I'm a guy who once rode the prairies of Oklahoma and North Texas in a green Buick and who slept in cheap motels and sold canary-yellow sport coats to store owners who sometimes stiffed me on the bill. I'm also a guy who built a $2.5 billion company, and who, on the day of our transfer to the New York Stock Exchange, got to ring the closing bell.

Some days were good, some were better than others, and they all came with a lesson. But the day that really stands out in my memory—the one that's got to be as good as any of them ever got—found me sitting in a golf cart on a perfect 85-degree day on the Big Island of Hawaii, smoking a joint with Neil Young.

Forgive me for the name-drop, but there is a point to the recollection of the moment in the cart, on the green-carpeted fairway, where I looked into a breathtaking expanse of blue sky and water and played a relaxed round of golf with one of the idols of my rock 'n' roll youth. It's more than just another peak experience from my past. It's when I was truly hit by the revelation of my life's most basic truth:

I am a fortunate son.

· · ·

My father and mother were both born in New York City, one a bookkeeper's son from Morningside Heights and the other the daughter of a prominent lawyer who was raised in a luxury Fifth Avenue apartment overlooking Central Park. I was born in New York City too: my folks had met, married, and moved to Stuyvesant Town a year before I was born in Doctors Hospital in 1948, but I can't remember a thing from my life in the high-rise apartments built on the Lower East Side for rising post-war middle-class urbanites. My folks moved out of the towers when I was four, with my younger brother Jimmy already on board and my sister Laurie in the planning stages. My

1

maternal grandfather put up the $5,000 down payment, and we moved into a $29,000 house in the suburb of Scarsdale. The same house is now worth $1.1 million. That was just the beginning of things that went right for me.

Robert Elkin Zimmer Jr., my father, was my number-one hero in life, and I'm proud to think that I was one of his, too. I broke into tears when he concluded the toast at my second wedding by turning to me and saying, "George, you're the best damn businessman I ever met."

Whatever success I've had in life pales in comparison to my father's foundational accomplishment: managing to stay alive during World War II. Drafted into the Army, he made first lieutenant and was assigned as a navigator on a B-24 bomber to the Fifteenth Air Wing that had about a 100 percent casualty rate. This was a kid who didn't even know how to drive a car.

My father probably didn't spend ten minutes talking to his children about his World War II experiences. We've only been able to assess them in yearbooks that my grandmother kept. They include letters my father wrote home, from his training days in Texas to his account of the European theater from his base in Foggia on the east coast of Italy, to his description of life in a Nazi prisoner-of-war camp.

"The bombing runs are very long, and we heavy bombers do not use any form of evasive action," he wrote his family after his flight team's tenth run, in plain, matter-of-fact language that betrays none of the terror that had to be coursing through him while he navigated through anti-aircraft fire and attacks from German fighter planes. "You've got to maintain formation, to pattern-bomb effectively. Thus, all we do is fly right through the flak come hell or high water. Over Vienna, the flak was so thick, it seemed like one huge black cloud. You see it burst, you can hear it hit the plane. And when you figure that just one of the bursts can rip you apart, you begin to think— and pray. You wait in agony for the bomb to drop because only then can you rally away from the flak . . . Sometimes a ship is hit so badly you have to crash land or bail out, sometimes they blow up in front of your eyes . . . You might eat breakfast with a guy and then see him spinning over the target."

On my dad's thirteenth mission, Nazi ground fire turned his plane into the horror show he described in his letter. Shot out of the sky over the oil fields outside of Vienna that fueled Hitler's war machine, my dad had the presence of mind while floating earthward in his parachute to rip off and throw away the dog tags that would have identified him as a Jew. Captured on the outskirts of Vienna, he was sent to a prisoner-of-war camp in Bavaria where he spent six months in captivity.

My father wrote in a neat, cursive script in his letters from Italy. Once he was shot down and captured, he switched to printing, an unspoken change that makes you think he suffered more than he spoke when he wrote to his mother and father, "Everything is moving along nicely in prison camp despite the inconveniences." He said he'd been reading, playing basketball, and attending "camp activities." Food, he wrote, "is an important item over here," and he asked his folks to send him coffee, sugar, and dehydrated soup.

"Remember Mom, Dad—I'm in the best of health and I'm happy. Rooming with a great bunch of boys helps a lot."

A little more than a month after that Nov. 16, 1944, letter, General George S. Patton's Third Army ended the Nazi siege at Bastogne and slogged onward into Germany, liberating my father's prisoner-of-war camp before pressing toward Berlin to end the war. My dad's letters told of hearing Patton's artillery thunder in the distance and mistaking the explosions for the sounds of our bombers, before they saw the American tanks crash through the fence line that surrounded the POW camp.

Back home in New York City, where he had grown up in an apartment on Riverside Drive at 110th Street, my father went to a 1946–47 New Year's Eve party where he met a Macy's sales clerk and University of Pennsylvania dropout. A year later, he married Marian Trosk in a ceremony at the Plaza Hotel.

How my mother gained entry into the world of Plaza Hotel weddings has remained a great family mystery, and the uncertainty of her origin has always fascinated and inspired me, while at the same time it has been a constant question mark in my life. The only thing we know for sure is that she was adopted as a baby out of a New York City orphanage. She never knew her biological mother, but according to family lore, a Ukrainian woman of Jewish origin fled her native country during the early years of the Soviet Union, in which tens of thousands of her people were slaughtered in the Stalinist pogroms. Somewhere between her overland flight from the steppe that stretched across the middle of the Eurasian land mass to the ship that took her across the sea to New York City, the woman, whose name we never knew, became pregnant. In America, she gave birth to a baby girl. Placed in the orphanage, my mother was adopted by one of the most prominent attorneys in Manhattan. His name was George Trosk, and he literally wrote the book on brief writing and appeals. The work is entitled *Brief Writing and Appeals*. You can buy it on Amazon for $851.

Governor Thomas Dewey once appointed my grandfather to head up a commission to investigate organized crime infiltration of pari-mutuel gambling in the state's harness racing tracks. "Papa George," as we called him, also represented the famed conductor Leopold Stokowski, best known for his collaboration with Walt Disney on *Fantasia*, in his high-society 1937 divorce from Johnson & Johnson heiress Evangeline Love Brewster Johnson. My grandfather was so good he was able to turn down a federal judgeship offered to him by Basil O'Connor, the former law partner and legal advisor to President Franklin D. Roosevelt. Papa George said he couldn't afford the pay cut.

Emotionally speaking, my mother and father were two completely different people—fire and ice. Who knows what they saw in each other, back at that New Year's party. My mother is the one who ran hot. She drank too much and could get extremely emotional. Call her unsettled, for lack of a better term. You could also call her smart, eccentric, witty, and adventurous. My theory is her restlessness stemmed from the mystery of her origin. She only had a vague idea about her birth mother and knew absolutely nothing about her biological father. Her family, wherever they were—were they all crazy? Were they geniuses? Gamblers or whores, or scientists or authors? I know the unknowns troubled her, from the conversations we had about it as I was growing up.

It's not that my father didn't express any emotion. But if his deadpan letters from the warfront are any indication, he just kept it sealed tight in the refrigerator of his inner being. He stayed inside himself, as you might expect from a man who had seen too much—growing up in the Depression, getting shot out of an airplane, and spending time in a prisoner-of-war camp. Back in our heyday, the Men's Wearhouse made a bio film on me where they interviewed my father. You can see there how he blankets his emotions. The interviewer asks him what he thinks about his kid, and whether he's proud of him, and my dad answers, "I'm surprised he became so successful." He was just reticent when it came to talking about how he felt. He never learned how to think with his heart.

My take on their marriage was, they wanted a family, and once they had one, they did the best they could to make their relationship work for the sake of their children. I think I'd have to conclude that they did not love each other, at least in the years that I can remember, and to that extent, their relationship was dysfunctional. They almost never fought with each other, at least not in front of me. It seemed to me that they did their best to make their marriage work—for us. They loved their children. They did the best they could for all three of us, and once we grew up and were out of the house, they got divorced.

• • •

My Scarsdale memories took shape beneath a canopy of green. Most people know Scarsdale Village for being a perennial top five in the listing of the wealthiest communities in America, or for its famous Scarsdale diet, or for the gunshot murder of its author, the cardiologist Dr. Herman Tarnower, who came up with the difficult-to-adhere-to, but effective, 1,000-calories-per-day eating plan. Perhaps just as famous as the diet itself is the love-triangle story that eventually led Dr. Tarnower's wife, Jean Harris, to do him in, an incident that dominated tabloid headlines for years.

But for me, the ingrained mental image of Scarsdale will always be its urban forest. Heritage beech and chestnut. Black cherry and walnut. Sycamore, swamp white oak, and shagbark hickory. Everywhere you rode on your bicycle, everywhere you walked, everywhere you played—you did it in the shade, in the green, at least during my favorite time of year, which was summer. In fall, the colors matched anything you'll ever see in New England. In winter, with the trees shorn of their cover, haunting images of branch and twig outlined against the gray sky could also take your breath away, before they blossomed fresh again in spring.

I played thousands of innings of Wiffle ball under those trees on the side of our second house, on Bethel Road. One of the massive trunks acted as both home plate and backstop. Any pitch that hit that tree was a strike, and anything you could launch into the trees on the other side of the yard went into the books as a home run.

I liked school and did pretty well in it, at least according to the notes scribbled on my report cards (every one of which my mother saved). "George has exhibited increasing self-confidence in his own ability, and his qualities of leadership are more and more apparent in various class discussions and group activities," my fifth-grade teacher at Greenacres Elementary School wrote. He saw something in me that I didn't quite see until many years later, when I got it into my head to start the Men's Wearhouse. Mr. (Hal) Baron also lauded me for "excellent work in the areas of Social Studies and Language Arts," a precursor of my lifetime concern about what's going on in America and the world. When it came to academics, I showed "consistent improvement" and demonstrated "considerably more concentration" as the academic years wore on. Reading through these comments today, in my seventies, I'm impressed by how closely these phrases echo the Japanese concept of kaizen, which loosely translates to "continuous improvement," and became the word I used for my business philosophy as soon as I learned the term.

Even in my tender years, the record shows I developed an aptitude for business. I worked my way up from my paper route for the *White Plains Reporter-Dispatch* to become the regional circulation manager by the time I hit high school. I rode the circuit by car to oversee the collections brought in by about sixty newsboys from all over Scarsdale. Mr. Baron also noted on one of my report cards that "George has done a fine job as one of the two managers of our School Store." I think this makes him the first to see that I had a future in retail.

• • •

I was hugely into sports as a kid. I wasn't especially talented at anything, but I played everything and loved it all: pick-up baseball, football, basketball, as well as a little tennis. Golf came later.

As much as anything, sports helped me bond with my dad. My father took us everywhere, to Yankee Stadium (my favorite), the Polo Grounds (not a big Giants fan), Ebbets Field (loved Dem Bums, until they moved west), and Shea Stadium (I was so-so on the Mets). At the old Madison Square Garden, we rooted for the Knicks and the Rangers, and I once saw Lew Alcindor play a high school game for Power Memorial before he became Kareem Abdul-Jabbar.

My favorite kid sports memories go back to the Columbia football games, even though the Lions usually finished toward the bottom of the Ivy League standings. Saturdays in the fall, you could always find us at the Columbia games—my father's alma mater, where he earned a business degree on the GI Bill. We'd sit in the stands at the old Baker Field on the banks of the Harlem River and sing "Roar, Lion, Roar," while Columbia usually lost. Except for 1961, when the blue-shirted Lions shocked the world when they won the Ivy title under Coach Aldo Donelli, with the Zimmer zealots in the stands. They haven't won one since.

Although I never had the physical tools to be a great athlete, there was something about the spirit of athletic competition that has always burned inside of me. Just about my whole life I brought it to every venue I entered, especially in business, and especially as CEO of the Men's Wearhouse, where I played hard and tough, and where I played to win, not just for myself, but for everybody on my team.

My father, though—he was a pretty good athlete himself. He'd take us to watch him play softball on Sundays in a men's league at the neighborhood schoolyard. He roamed center field and batted third, although not everybody took the games as seriously as he did—I remember guys smoking cigars while they played first base.

My mother also had her hobbies. She liked to drive fast cars and fly airplanes. Like I said earlier, she also liked to drink. Sometimes, she liked to fly *and* drink. Usually, she'd take a bottle of scotch along as her copilot. Not surprisingly, she mostly flew alone, sometimes just for the experience, sometimes to family events like college graduations. The rest of us drove.

My mother's drinking sometimes led to erratic behavior. As kids, we always had to think twice before we brought a friend over to the house. You never knew which mother you were going to get when you got home from school. Sometimes, you got normal mom, who was friendly and talkative. Sometimes, you got lunatic mom—eccentric and unpredictable. We used to tease her sometimes when she got sloshed, and you never knew how she'd react. One time she picked up a dish and threw it at me. She'd just bought a whole set and they were supposed to be unbreakable. Ha! The plate missed me and smashed into a thousand pieces when it hit the wall, which gave us all a pretty good laugh, although it makes me a little sad to remember it now. And there was nothing funny about the tension her inability to manage her booze created between her and my father.

Don't get me wrong about my mom. Same as everybody, she was a complex human being who could be good, bad, or ugly. And same as it should be for everybody, nobody ever loved me more, or so unconditionally. Nobody ever provided me with more encouragement, or support. She instilled in me a belief that I could do anything I wanted in life, could accomplish anything I wanted to, be any person that I wanted to be. Nobody did more to boost my confidence. I was her firstborn, and I think I was her favorite among the three of us kids. At least I felt I was the favorite, as every child should, and that gave me a feeling that whatever I did was going to turn out all right, and I carried that belief within myself all my life.

I wouldn't say that she was an optimistic person, but she sure made me one. She gave me a sense that if I gave anything my best, it would turn out all right, and that was a spirit that allowed me to take some of the chances that worked out pretty well for me later in life.

More than anyone else, despite the fact that my dad was the business guy, she gave me the faith in myself to launch my own company, to make it grow, to make it great.

The two of them, for whatever their imperfections, set me up for the long haul of life with love and support, a sense of the idyllic, and plenty of good fortune.

• • •

Some of my best memories growing up had my brother and me accompanying my father on his job. Decades before anybody ever heard of "take-your-kid-to-work day," my dad packed the two of us up to accompany him when he made his rounds on weekends as a vice president for Robert Hall Clothes. This was the big men's clothing chain that did pretty well around New York, Chicago, and Los Angeles during the fifties and sixties. He signed on with them right out of college as a $35-a-week stock boy. Sure as he made it out alive from a blown-up B-24 bomber, he was promoted through the Robert Hall hierarchy.

On non-football Saturdays, his job took him out on the road to personally check out stores in the tristate area. My brother and I had a blast playing hide-and-seek in the coat racks, on the car trips that took us from Stamford to Yonkers to Teaneck. The best part was once he finished his business, he took the three of us out to lunch, and usually in some fun place where they had those electronic bowling machines.

Somehow, the Robert Hall moments—the smell and feel of the clothes on the racks, the sight of tailors doing their work and satisfied customers walking away with a garment bag over their shoulders—must have sealed themselves into my unconscious, because they later emerged in the very layout of the Men's Wearhouse. Our first Men's Wearhouse store, and all our early stores when we became a small chain in Houston, we consciously laid out on the Robert Hall model. The idea: huge volume, low cost, and no frills, for men who just wanted to get in and get out as quickly as they could. Linoleum floors and metal pipe racks on wheels—step right up, buy the one suit you're going to own for the next ten years, and be on your way.

If the Robert Hall model provided half of the idea for me to become a men's apparel merchant, my father provided the other half when he quit the chain to go into business for himself, about the time I was a freshman in high school. He left Robert Hall to create his own raincoat manufacturing business for boys. He called it Royalad Apparel, later to be renamed Zimco Industries. I worked for him all through high school, driving a truck over the summers and picking up garments at his three factories in Connecticut and transporting them to his warehouse. Making the runs, I'd dig on the AM radio hits of the day like Sam the Sham and the Pharaohs' "Wooly Bully" and the Lovin' Spoonful's "Summer in the City," a couple of my favorites.

I remember one day in November 1963, when my dad damn near jumped out of his chair at the sight of something on TV. The occasion was John F. Kennedy's funeral. Perhaps the most searing visual of the day occurred when the camera turned to the assassinated president's three-year-old son and the little boy snapped off a salute to the carriage that contained the casket of his slain father. While my father wept with America, he also exclaimed about John-John's attire, "My God—he's wearing our coat!" The most royal lad in the country was wearing my father's clothes.

• • •

My mother taught me that with wealth came obligation. She was president of a service organization called Vacation Camp for the Blind. They'd run people to dances and such at neighborhood American Legion halls and up to the Catskills for two-week breaks from summer in the city. When I got old enough to drive, she signed me up to chauffer blind people to summer camp.

She gave me the keys to her car and addresses and directions to the homes of Westchester County's poor, mostly in apartment buildings, where I would knock on the clients' doors and drive them to wherever we were going.

Most of the people I picked up were African American. I'd be lying if I said it wasn't scary to go into some of those buildings in some of the tougher corners of Westchester County, of which there were a few. Race riots had already begun to break out and the tension between white and Black in New York City and across America had grown pretty thick. But the people were extremely appreciative of what we were doing, and it didn't take long for their neighbors to approve of the white boy from Scarsdale, too.

These visions of poverty exposed me for the first time in my life to the reality of income and wealth inequality, and how it disproportionately affected Black people, at least in the corner of the world I grew up in. I mean, you didn't need to be a sociologist to see the 1964 disparity between Scarsdale and some of the poorer neighborhoods of Yonkers. Most of the people I drove around were on Social Security, and most of the people I encountered in their neighborhoods lived on less than that. Poverty up close hit me right in the mouth. I didn't yet know what to make of what I was seeing and learning.

Neither my mother nor my father was particularly political. But if anything from my youth shaped the progressive politics that I would embrace as an adult, I'd sure have to say that this exposure to inequality pried my eyes wide open. It was one thing to read about the issues in the *New York Times* or the *White Plains Reporter-Dispatch*. It was a whole other thing to see it up close, even in Westchester County, and I have my mother's social sense to thank.

I would have so much more to thank her for in the future, including her generosity that saved me and the Men's Wearhouse from financial ruin.

· · ·

All four of my grandparents played large roles in raising and shaping me. In effect, I had six parents, another part of my life's good fortune. We visited one set of grandparents or the other pretty much every weekend, at my father's folks' middle-class apartment on Riverside Drive at 110th Street or my mother's parents' place with the multimillion-dollar view of Central Park.

Papa Al—my dad's dad—lost a business during the Depression and never seemed to get over it. He counted other people's money as a book-keeper for thirty years before he retired and then died with a chip on his shoulder when I was in high school. Maybe he never reached his potential as a businessman, but he sure did know his numbers. I think my own proficiency at arithmetic came from being around him, some of it in the form of playing gin. His wife, my grandmother, Nana Jessie, was an incredibly sweet lady. Her warmth made up for Papa Al's gruff demeanor. Anytime I'd go into a funk, she knew how to retrieve me from the brink, with a bowl of the chocolate ice cream she always kept in the freezer. "George," she used to tell me when I'd ask her if too much chocolate ice cream was bad for you, "chocolate ice cream is never bad for you."

Nana Jessie also had her own theatrical costume business. I remember her lugging boxes of ensembles on city buses. She got to know producers, theater managers—everybody, and she parlayed those contacts into the best seats in the house on Broadway. And I do mean the best: four, in the fourth-row center. The theaters kept them in reserve in the event that President Eisenhower, Kennedy, or Johnson, or any one of their friends or relatives, ever wanted to catch a show. When they didn't, Nana Jessie somehow worked her way onto the list to fill them. I don't remember missing anything I really wanted to see. My loving Nana and these trips to Broadway gave me my sense of fun. I'd like to think I picked up some schtick from all those Broadway plays when it came time to go on TV for the Men's Wearhouse, and of course the transformative role of costume, in theater and the real world, was not lost on someone who came to be a big player in the garment industry.

On my mother's side, things were more formal. Papa George and Nana Gertie had maids and servants. Dinner at their house came out in courses, right down to the creamed herring and chopped chicken liver (which I loved). Nana Gertie died fairly young. Papa George, in her absence, wore a black tie every day for the rest of his life. Our weekends with him shifted to our house. He'd take the train up to Scarsdale and hang with the kids pretty much every weekend. He had his own bedroom in our house.

On Saturday nights, my mother and father usually went out to dinner or some other event with their friends. My brother and sister and I would then eat dinner with Papa George, a meal that he always capped with a shot of bourbon. Jimmy and Laurie would then take off to go hang out with their friends, and I would stay home and listen to Papa George's stories about the law. He had a million of 'em. If you don't believe me, Google him.

Papa George was a fairly conservative guy. As liberal as I am, my memories of my grandfather have always underlined the need for counterbalance.

I've always believed that compassion and empathy must stand side by side with accountability and hard work. Papa George gave me the accountability and hard work part. He also passionately believed that the rule of law stood above all else in a civilized society. I would later ask, whose law, and for whom, but I understood that Papa George was talking about standards and rules that everybody had to live by, without favor or preference. Even though he was conservative, he showed me what he meant when he told me, years later, that he voted for Jimmy Carter against Gerald Ford in the 1976 presidential election, solely on the basis of Ford pardoning Richard Nixon, who my grandfather thought was, in fact, a crook.

My grandfather preached integrity above all else. No matter who you were or what you did, if you were honest and upright, you would always have your sense of self-respect, which would keep you fighting into the next round. It was something, in his view, that you always had to hold, even when nobody was looking and the stakes were small—like me, driving him somewhere and going fifty miles per hour when the speed limit said forty-five. He'd call me on it. And, when my dad had his own business, Papa George used to protest when my dad paid for dinner on his company credit card. My dad would laugh it off, as if it all came out in the wash. Papa George thought the tax implications of a business versus a personal expense mattered, right down to the penny.

Looking back, I can see how the six distinct personalities and characteristics of my mother, my father, and my four grandparents shaped me into the person I became. They were all honest, and they worked hard, and they were smart. They had high standards, and they exposed me to different values that made me think about the world outside of myself, made me think about others, and as an adult, made me aware that in business, there was a hell of a lot more to success than just making money.

• • •

Coming from a white, upper-middle-class, Jewish family sure had its advantages. One of the best was when I was thirteen and my folks sent me off on a train tour of North America, in the summer of '62—my coming of age.

My parents sent me on the trip with my best friend, Charlie Bresler, another kid from Scarsdale who lived eight houses away from me. Some thirty years later, long after we fell out of contact, Charlie, who by then had become a big-shot psychologist, saw me in a TV ad and called me on the phone. I ended up hiring him into the Men's Wearhouse, and he eventually became our president.

Charlie and I called the train trip the "Teen Tour." Along the way, the two of us learned to play bridge, which gave me an outlet for my competitive spirit. I think it was by playing bridge that I first learned that I'm an alpha male. Some of the skills that go into being a good bridge player—being able to intuitively read your partner's moves, and being able to see multiple developments taking place at the same time—would later serve me hugely in business. Charlie and I, we turned into a real good team. By the time we circled the country, nobody on the train could beat us. We maintained our partnership all the way through high school, a pair of nerdish teenagers who kicked ass in local tournaments.

First up on the Teen Tour was a ride across Canada on the Canadian Pacific Railway, from Winnipeg to Vancouver. Then, a border crossing to Seattle and down the West Coast, to San Francisco, and over to Yosemite National Park. The wonder of granite and falling water spoke for itself, but what really stuck in my mind and heart was meeting a girl on the valley floor. Under the expanse of the Milky Way and spread out over the hood of a car, I enjoyed the splendor of my first kiss.

Next stop, Los Angeles, and a couple of nights at the Ambassador Hotel, where Bobby Kennedy would be assassinated six years later. Our group scored some tickets to a happening in the Cocoanut Grove, the hotel's famous nightclub, but Charlie and I had other plans. We wanted to go see a baseball game in the new stadium that opened that year in Chavez Ravine. No car, no problem—we were New Yorkers, and we knew how to take the bus. The chaperones gave us our ten bucks that was supposed to go toward the fancy night in the ballroom. We used the cash to pay for the bus fare and a pair of seventy-five-cent seats in the right-field bleachers, with plenty left over for hot dogs and Cokes.

Out of L.A., we rumbled across the desert tracks to the West Texas town of El Paso where we fell in love with *Lawrence of Arabia*, which we saw on the big screen in a downtown theater. Across the south, we reached destination Miami where we boarded a cruise ship for a three-day tour of the Bahamas. In port at Nassau, I experienced another first—my first drunk. They'd stocked our room on the cruise ship with a lineup of minis. I chose the Harveys Bristol Cream, my Nana Jessie's favorite.

Booze would later become a problem for me, just like it was for my mother. I had no problem, however, giving it up when I knew it was time. I got off the sauce easy enough, with the help of a different type of medicine that I had come to try and would continue to enjoy over the years—marijuana.

• • •

I wish that everybody could be a fortunate son or daughter. I wish that everybody could be raised in the same kind of family cocoon that gave me the chance to create a successful business. I wish that everybody could see the Yankees, tour the country, and even get a sense of the wider world at the ripe old age of thirteen.

Of course, I worked hard—you can't accomplish anything without sacrifice and effort. I also did come up with that catchy slogan that people still greet me with on the street or at sporting events where I now live in Oakland. Maybe I did have some innate talent and smarts, and maybe my competitive spirit drove me to succeed in ways that you couldn't if you weren't an alpha male (or female). I for sure am a guy who came up with good idea at a good time and a good place. I also like to think that I'm a decent human being, and that good karma matters.

Even if all of the above is true—and it is—the fact remains that there are billions of people in this world who assuredly are just as decent, who work just as hard, who are just as driven, and who are just as smart. Still, they were never able to create their own businesses. Their faces never invaded television sets from coast to coast and they weren't fortunate enough to buy a second home in Hawaii.

What did I have that they lacked? The answer I always come back to is my good fortune.

By the accident of birth, I was delivered into a solid and supportive post–World War II nuclear family headed by greatest-generation parents who gave me confidence as well as opportunity at a time when my country was at the height of its international influence and economic greatness. I was fortunate that my parents had the resources to raise me in an idyllic social and physical environment. I was fortunate that they conditioned me to expect the best, from myself and from everybody I met.

Maybe I was most fortunate that they sent me off to one of the finest universities in the world, in the decade when people my age—in all our self-regard—considered ourselves the vanguard of enlightened societal transformation, to liberate the country out of war and racism and stagnant thinking.

We thought we could reshape the world.

→ 2 ←

Come Together

Fall semester of my senior year at Washington University, the Beatles released their second-to-last album, *Abbey Road*. As I'd done for *Sgt. Pepper's* and *The White Album* and *Yellow Submarine*, I got together with a half dozen of my college pals. We hosed up to the hookah and stuffed it up with the best pot you could find those days on the streets of St. Louis, or through my friends' connections back in their hometowns. Then we proceeded to blow our minds.

Not once, not twice, but with several play-throughs of each song on each album, we engaged in lengthy discussions to discern meanings hidden and apparent in every verse. We exulted in the pure joy of rock 'n' roll, as well as the spirit trip that the Beatles were taking us on. The rightness of the music, for us and for the times, opened our minds to what was going on in the collective unconscious. We knew that something was happening here, even if it wasn't exactly clear. We knew it was revolutionary. We knew we were in the middle of it.

The Vietnam War. The civil rights movement. The explosion of the ghettos. The assassinations of Martin Luther King, Jr., and Bobby Kennedy. Bank burnings and ROTC fire bombings. Pipe bombings on Wall Street and in the Capitol Building. A blown-up townhouse in Greenwich Village. Riots, protests, street marches, and demonstrations. The Weather Underground. The Black Panther Party, the Brown Berets, and the American Indian Movement. All of it played to a soundtrack supplied by the Beatles, Jimi and Janis, Sly and the Family Stone, Dylan and the Dead, and Neil Young. Woodstock gave way to Altamont, upstate New York's orgy of free love turned inside out by Hell's Angels violence that shattered our sense that we had created a brave new world. We read *Be Here Now* and *Steal This Book*, and we tracked our own coming of age to *Siddhartha*. *The Graduate* told the story of our lives, even if most of us never got it on with the neighbor lady. Every town had an alternative newspaper and a freak radio station. Zap

Comics introduced America to "White Man," who fretted that he "must maintain this rigid posture or all is lost." Muhammad Ali showed that you cannot separate sport from society.

The movies, the music—even the heavyweight champion of the world—it all came together during the latter half of the 1960s in a sweeping movement that affected every aspect of American life. We called it "the counterculture," which we roughly defined as a new way of thinking and acting and relating that represented a serious departure from the evolution of America in the post–World War II years.

By definition, it came about in reaction to what had been the American way of life. A social and political gathering, the general feeling among the counterculture was that the United States just didn't have everything quite right.

Nobody could doubt the greatness of a country that saved the world from Hitler and created an economy that allowed huge segments of ordinary working-class people to buy their own homes, send their children to college, and retire in dignity. Maybe we didn't appreciate those things enough when we were young. All we knew is that there was so much more that needed to be done to make the society work for everybody. We also knew that in some key places in the world, like in Vietnam and in the American South, things had gone (or stayed) terribly wrong. We thought that the hubris of the American military-industrial mindset needed to be checked.

On our side, we sought to shake America out of an inertia that had allowed it to stray from its founding principles. We looked to bring back the national spirit that defeated slavery, regulated big business, organized unions, and challenged Jim Crow. Like in those movements of great change, the time had come, as we saw it, for us to make sure everyone was bestowed freedom and dignity. We saw it as our cause to let America know that it had a long way to go to form the more perfect union.

Politics had exploded all around us, almost from the time we all landed at Washington University, which we considered to be the Berkeley of the Midwest. Right around the same time as *Abbey Road*'s release, I marched to Washington, DC, with five hundred thousand peaceniks, radicals, liberals, and hippies such as ourselves, all aligned against the Vietnam War. I helped occupy the administration building at Wash U., itself a hotbed of radical thought and activity just like the West Coast Berkeley. I watched cops file off a bus and beat college girls over the head with billy clubs.

Like the decade did to millions of others, the sixties turned my head around, right there at Wash U., where I gladly gave in to new sensibilities. I found that despite the comfortable, even idyllic circumstances of my childhood, I was open to change. I tried to align myself with a purpose. I came to *believe* things before I saw them, which is the exact opposite of the old adage I heard from my parents a million times that seeing is believing.

Decades later, I came to realize that the sixties represented a battle between love and fear. I didn't read *The Prince* until more than a decade into the next century, in which Machiavelli famously wrote that with all things being equal, for political (and, in my case, business) leaders, it's better to be feared than to be loved—that is, if they intended to preserve their own power. Now, in retrospect, I would say that the sixties were all about trying to prove Machiavelli wrong.

I am not so naive as to think that this world isn't a fearful place. There is plenty to be afraid of. But I believe that the sixties gave us a glimpse into how love can trump fear, in some ways small, in our personal lives, and some ways large, such as ending a genocidal war. We believed in the change, and then we saw it.

The sixties certainly shaped me into what I ultimately became.

More than a half a century later, I still get a kick from looking back at my college days, and at the strands of my life that I picked up and wove together in the sixties, at Washington University, that have remained strong, that still run through me, that still define me.

. . .

As fondly as I recall my childhood, the truth is that I couldn't wait to move away from it. By the time I finished Scarsdale High School, I had to get out of town. Maybe it was just the rebellious streak that hits so many teenagers at the onset of early adulthood. I needed to find out who I was, and the only way I could embark on the journey of self-discovery was to leave the comfort of my familiar surroundings. To be honest, though my father had so much of my respect and a high level of influence in my life, I was something of a mama's boy. I figured that Wash U. was as good a place as any find my own way.

My top college pick—the University of Pennsylvania—turned me down, which didn't fluster me too much, and the second school on my list,

Occidental College out in Los Angeles, wait-listed me, which was okay, too, the way it turned out. Again, I just needed to get out, and at that point it didn't matter to me too much where. Wisconsin and Case Western Reserve also accepted me, but I went with the Ivy League feel of Wash U. My junior year in high school, my father took me out to St. Louis the weekend of George Washington's birthday to see the school. It's a big day at the name-sake university, and I liked the festiveness. I also liked, and grew to love, St. Louis. Wash U. turned out to be the perfect place for me, and has remained a big part of who I am.

As far as what I hoped to accomplish in my college years, I had a vague belief that I'd probably go into business. But to tell the truth, I really didn't have any academic goals or any motivation to pursue a particular course of study. I'd be fine with a collection of gentleman's Cs and Bs. Maybe it was naivete on my part, but when I was a freshman in college, I'd felt I'd already done all my academic heavy lifting in high school. The only thing I really needed to learn was whether I could become a fully functioning adult male.

It wouldn't be completely incorrect to say that when I went off to Wash U., I was something of a geek, at least when it came to girls. I mean, I certainly was no ladies' man in high school, or an athlete, or a hipster, or any-thing that would have made me noticeable. I did very well with the books, and stayed busy and out of trouble. My favorite hobby was playing bridge. No disrespect to the game—I loved it then and I still do now—but it wasn't exactly something that would get you laid.

Off into my St. Louis testing ground, I was free to reinvent myself into anything I wanted, and at that point, one thing I really wanted to accom-plish was to figure out how to get over with girls. I was kind of shy and uncertain about myself, fearful of rejection. I don't think I ever had a date in high school, and that was a gap in my experience that I sought to fill. I decided the new college self that I was breaking in wouldn't be shy about asking girls out. My first date was with the daughter of one of my college professors. I put on a coat and tie—what do you expect from the son of a men's clothing merchant from New York, where men young and old wore the goddamn things to baseball games? I went to her house to pick her up, and she greeted me in sneakers and capris. To say I was overdressed would be an understatement. I would eventually figure these things out.

Working my way around the Wash U. campus, I took every opportunity to meet and date as many girls as I could. Somewhere along my journey of growing up, I had come to understand this to be extremely important to becoming the fully functioning adult male.

Another high priority was to find my tribe. Though I was undeniably loved at home, my father was quiet and my mother unpredictable. In high school, I had remained somewhat aloof, didn't glom on to any of the groups you found there. The three Jewish fraternities on the Washington University campus seemed to be beacons of community to a young adult in search of identity, and the connection I made with the Sigma Alpha Mu fraternity guided me wonderfully through my four years in St. Louis.

I pledged with a kid from Dallas named Harry Levy who would turn out to be one of my best friends, in life and in business. I think Harry's the first person I ever smoked pot with, and there's something about the company you share the first time you get stoned that stays with you. There's a bonding there, in the altered and alternative and very real new perspective that marijuana lends to life and the world.

Harry was a big guy who, like me, loved sports—he played blocking back on our intramural flag-football team. (I was a linebacker, and my senior year, I coached the team—I guess I was learning that I had serious leadership qualities.) Of course, Harry became a regular at the hookah parties, and he and I shared a lifelong love of the Moody Blues, maybe my favorite band of all time—we never missed a show in St. Louis and we caught them several more times over the years when we became real live grown-ups, all the way through to the final time we saw them in 2013 in San Francisco, a couple of years before Harry died.

The dude was a flat-out computer genius with a Mensa-level intellect. Harry didn't have rich parents or grandparents, and he had to work his way through college. He got himself a graveyard gig with Honeywell in St. Louis. I used to bring him pizzas in the middle of the night at his job, and he'd show me around the Honeywell mainframes, which took up an entire floor of office space. He'd gone high tech before anybody had ever heard of the term.

A few years out of college, Harry came up with $3,000 to become the first outside investor in the Men's Wearhouse. He helped me come up with the name, even before we opened our first store in Houston in 1973. Later on, he installed the groundbreaking computer system that helped us become one of the first companies in the world to link our supply chain to the point of sale.

• • •

From our earliest days at Sigma Alpha Mu, Harry and everybody else in our pledge class, and in the rest of the fraternity, for that matter, came to know and love me a little better through a very key person in my life—my mother.

I don't think I ever felt more liberated in my life than when my mother, who flew out to St. Louis with me to set me up in my dorm, hugged me goodbye and finally let me be on my own. Same as the over-involved moms of nowadays, my mother helicoptered over my life to the point of domineering it. Sometimes, she came on like one of those fighters that protected my father's B-24 on his World War II bombing runs.

Wouldn't you know it, the day came early in my freshman year when I was never happier to see her: when I suffered the medical calamity of a twisted testicle. It happens when one of those guys down there rotates the wrong way and your spermatic cord winds up tied in a knot. The pain is severe, and surgery is required. My mother flew out the night of the operation in the amphitheater of the Barnes Hospital on the Wash U. medical campus, while a dozen or so med students watched from the bleachers. She took care of me while I was in the hospital, and after my release, she stuck around while I recovered.

While I was laid, up, she spent a lot of time with my frat brothers. They dug her, and they sort of adopted her as the frat-house mom, a position that she held for the next four years. The brothers' affection for her also cascaded over me in my first year in the house. Somehow, this made it all come full circle for me—my mom accepting my new family, and my frat brothers digging her, made me feel like I was on the right path to finding out who I was. At least a dozen times over the next four years, she and my father came out for Sigma Alpha Mu parties. With rock 'n' roll music blaring from the stereo, my mother showed the boys that she knew her way around the dance floor. From a distance, you'd never know she represented a different generation.

I really liked it when they came out, and my memories of them at the frat parties probably rank with the best mental pictures that I have of them together. But it was in that first year in college, seeing them in my new environment, that I became more intellectually aware of the problems in their marriage that lent an overlay of tension to my upbringing. I could see it even at the frat parties, how she let it all hang out on the dance floor, while my father played from a distance. It also became clear to me at the parties the different ways in which alcohol affected—and even controlled—my mother. I'm sure it was in those years that I first developed my own problems with the stuff. Coming out of an adolescence of stone sobriety, in college I often found myself bombed on booze, even before I discovered the miracle of pot. It took me a long time before I realized that I needed to stop drinking—which I did in 1981, and haven't had a drink since.

Anyway, it was in college that I first really saw the dysfunction in their relationship that led to their eventual divorce. My father would eventually meet and marry another woman, a relationship that lasted for more than forty years until his death. My mother never remarried.

Despite my complicated relationship with her, for some reason I think I needed my mother to come check out my scene my freshman year at Wash U. I think I needed her approval, needed her to give me a thumbs up or thumbs down on my new path. She gave it to me on that first visit to St. Louis for my surgery, telling me she thought Wash U. was maybe the perfect social environment for me. It gave me a massive confidence boost. Weird as it sounds, maybe I'm the type of guy who needed my mother's validation to achieve my goal of becoming a fully functioning adult male.

Thanks to her, and to my fraternity brothers, and to the fact that I'd truly started on the long journey of figuring out women (still unfinished), by the time summer rolled around, I felt I'd racked up an A in the subject of getting my feet wet. I slid right into a strong, fraternity-based social life. I'd bonded with a best buddy with whom I would build a business and know and love for forty-nine years. I even learned that you didn't necessarily need to wear a tie to impress the girls on first dates. The rest of my frat brothers and I—especially the twenty-five who pledged in the fall of '66—we wrapped each other in a nice, tight cocoon that first year in St. Louis. Academically speaking, I successfully achieved my goal of maintaining a C average.

I didn't know it when I first landed on campus, but there was another Jewish frat boy at another Jewish fraternity at Wash U., a contemporary of mine who later did pretty well for himself named Harold Ramis. He was a couple years older than me and had joined up with Zeta Beta Tau. The Ghostbuster who was also one of America's all-time great comedy writers— the genius who teamed up with a collection of other geniuses to write *Animal*

House. I'm sure Ramis came up with an idea for a character in the film off a guy in my fraternity. Harold never specifically copped to it, at least not to me when we met decades later, but neither did he tell me that the chopper-up-the-stairway tough guy who played the "William Tell Overture" by flicking his throat with his fingers *wasn't* Harvey Krasilovsky, a member of my pledge class.

They called him "D-Day" in the movie. The real-life Kras, as we used to call him, was a kid from Long Island who got a football scholarship at a big-time college but suffered a career-ending injury and ultimately transferred to Wash U. Like the guy in the movie, Kras carried himself around campus as somebody you did not want to fuck with. He cut his shirt sleeves up to the shoulder to expose those massive upper arms that could lay you out in a second. We were happy to have him on our side, even if his football injuries were so severe that he couldn't even play on our frat-house intramural team. Our "D-Day" prototype actually *did* ride his Harley up the stairs from the basement and then up another flight to a mid-landing, just like the guy did in the movie. In the *Animal House* epilogue, D-Day speeds off in a stolen police car to a future of "whereabouts unknown." The real Kras became a psychiatrist.

I experimented with tobacco and alcohol and overindulged in both, even though I didn't really like either of them. I guess that's just part of college, to do things that you've never done before, the things that the older generation may have warned you against. College is maybe the one time in life where you can really be out there. You're not buried yet in your commitments to your career, or anything else. You are allowed to be crazy—it's almost even expected of you. For a kid like me who grew up in a safety net, you can take risks for maybe the first time in your life. You can experiment with danger. You can smoke and drink, and I forced myself into trying both in college. Still, I played it pretty conservatively my first year in St. Louis, a rookie in life, away from home for the first time. I was into toga parties, not the Youth International Party.

I did notice the literature tables around campus, meant to fill your head with new thoughts and ideas and positions and perspectives. I didn't pay a whole lot of attention until my sophomore year.

Year Two at Wash U., that's when I began to learn about the Vietnam War and the civil rights movement. The latter had gained greater urgency by the time I got to St. Louis, with riots burning in the ghettos from coast to coast after the assassination of Dr. Martin Luther King, Jr. I became aware of environmentalism, beyond the national anti-littering advertising campaigns. Wash U., in fact, served as something of an epicenter for the international environmental movement, thanks to Professor Barry Commoner, an internationally renowned plant physiologist and a 1980 presidential candidate on the Citizens Party ticket. Dr. Commoner launched his Center for the Biology of Natural Systems the same year that I enrolled in St. Louis. Like thousands of other Wash U. students, I attended his extremely popular classes on the interconnectedness of life.

All of these causes, they demanded your attention, and I gave them mine. When I returned to St. Louis for my sophomore year, we were coming off the Summer of Love. The sixties were on, and I jumped into them.

• • •

I can't say that I was on the vanguard of this American cultural revolution that fell under the umbrella that we called "the counterculture." As I said, I barely noticed it my freshman year. Sophomore year, however, I couldn't shut it out, and I didn't want to. By the time I returned to St. Louis for my second fall semester, the Summer of Love had come and stayed, especially on college campuses across America. The war in Vietnam escalated, and with it, campus activism to stop it. My favorite bands got more politicized and psychedelicized. My mind was open to *anything*. I became an active listener, an original member of the audience that dug Abbie Hoffman, Bobby Seale, and John Lennon and the radical concepts that they professed.

Remember the book that came out a few decades ago by Robert Fulghum, *All I Really Need to Know I Learned in Kindergarten?* Well, for me, all I really needed to understand the world, I learned through the counterculture. It gave me an analytical perspective that I've never dropped.

I came to believe then, and I still think now, that we need a reordering of so much that is going on in America. Too many people in power are consumed by money and property and shareholder value. Over the decades, I've worked to reorder our priorities, at least at the scale of my own business and to the extent I could in larger arenas, to place a higher emphasis on human life. A business needs to think about the interests of everybody else in society, not just their investors and shareholders. My second year of college, my fundamental belief system changed when it came to America. I thought mainstream culture was superficial. Countercultural thinking impelled millions of us to work to create change, whether it was to become political activists or create food co-ops or just raise your children to think about more than themselves. The counterculture gave us values that way outlived the sixties. In my case, it incited me to create a business that shared the wealth with our workers, understood and valued our customers, and made fair deals with our suppliers.

Same as it is now, you had to pick a tribe. I chose the one that marched against the war and for civil rights, the one that was re-examining every aspect of American life: what we ate, what we watched on TV, what we listened to on the radio, how we related to each other. Everything was on the table then, and it still is today. Something was wrong with America then, and I think something is terribly wrong now with a country that could elect Donald Trump as its president.

While I embraced the revolution, I never turned my back on frat life, or the frat crowd largely made up of more conservative students whom I still considered my friends. I'm sure it was my deep respect and admiration for my father's bravery and heroism in World War II that kept me from ever blaming our troops for the fiasco in Vietnam. At the same time, I got to know and like and hang out with campus radicals and other left-wing groups, not to mention the pot smokers.

I came to consider myself the campus liaison between the freaks and the straights. And in the decades since, I've tried to serve as a bridge between their different ways of thinking and living.

By the time the spring semester of my sophomore year rolled around, my bushy brown hair had spread down my shoulders and up and around into a halo over my head. I'd become a full-on hippie.

I think I got part of the way there through my fascination with marijuana. I can't remember the exact time when I first got high with Harry Levy, although I'm pretty sure it was sometime in the fall of '67. The main thing about pot, for me, was that it just made everything really funny. First it was just Harry and me, then a few more of our frat brothers, and then we found a wider brotherhood of potheads, and we started the hookah parties for whenever the Beatles or the Moody Blues or the Grateful Dead or Jefferson Airplane popped a new album. Or we'd throw on something by the piano-playing, social-satirizing comic Tom Lehrer, or by the Firesign Theater, and we'd all collapse into uncontrollable laughter, or somebody in the group would bust everybody up with some kind of remark or observation that the next day nobody could remember.

It was like I'd found my consciousness-alteration niche. It was nontoxic, or at least less toxic, and certainly noncaloric as long as you controlled the urge to munch. It opened my mind and gave me an enhanced view of music and art and sports and literature. There's no doubt that it played a central role in the spread of countercultural thinking, mine and the rest of my generation's. Not that it was a religious or spiritual experience or anything, in and of itself, but it did help me feel and perceive things in a different way.

• • •

My politics had never been fully formed at home, where my parents only rarely discussed them. We weren't one of those families that argued the pressing issues of the day around the dinner table. I can't even tell you for sure how they voted. I'm pretty sure they were Republican, although they never made a fuss about it. I think they voted for John F. Kennedy against Richard M. Nixon in the 1960 presidential election—they liked the "new generation" feel that JFK presented to the country. Again, I don't know, but I think they went with Lyndon B. Johnson over Barry Goldwater in 1964—I just can't say for sure. Politics simply never dominated conversation in our household. Not that they were anti-politics, or uninterested. Politics just weren't that big a deal, between my dad running a business and my mother flying off into the wild blue yonder with a fifth of scotch at her side. I think this was more common at the time than it is today—politics were something separate that you could decide to be interested in or not, unlike now, when they can color almost every aspect of who you are.

At Wash U., with sixties progressivism breaking out all over, I developed a solid liberal framework for my worldview. In the 1968 presidential campaign, I found a politician who for the first time stimulated my political passion. I liked everything I knew about Bobby Kennedy. I'd always viewed him as good on civil rights, and I thought his plan for getting us out of Vietnam made sense. Today's Bernie Sanders Democrats probably wouldn't have liked his proposal for a phased withdrawal, which ran up against the unequivocal, end-the-war-now insistence of Kennedy's main rival for the progressive vote, Minnesota Senator Eugene McCarthy. No matter—Bobby Kennedy was my guy, and I rooted for him throughout the spring, once he entered the race when LBJ dropped out after the incumbent's less-than-overwhelming performance in the New Hampshire primary. (Nobody really cared about the Iowa caucuses in those days.)

A couple of hours after midnight, St. Louis time, on the night of June 4, 1968, after his successful California primary, I watched Bobby's victory speech at the Ambassador Hotel in Los Angeles, the same place that I visited on my "Teen Tour" as a thirteen-year-old. I guess that gave me more of a feel when Bobby stepped to the podium after he won the primary and declared, "Now it's on to Chicago and let's win there." I'd never been more fired up about politics in my life, watching the only politician up to that time that I'd ever truly cared about, when he flashed that thumbs-up to the crowd while his wife, Ethel, smiled.

I watched as the gargantuan football player Rosey Grier ushered Bobby through the curtains behind the podium. Then, just a few minutes later, the TV news anchors, after a weirdly silent delay, reported that Bobby Kennedy had been shot. I stayed with the story all night long from the frat house at Wash U., and then all the next day and night, for twenty-six hours straight, hanging on every update, every commentary, until the announcement came at 1:44 AM West Coast time that the third American progressive leader in less than five years had been shot and killed by assassins who to this day have remained subjects of mystery and conspiracy theories (some of which I think are true).

To me, Bobby Kennedy's murder represented the death of hope. It hit me like nothing I'd ever felt before in my life. To this day, it's one of the most traumatic things I've ever experienced. Coming just two months after the shooting death of Dr. Martin Luther King, Jr., and only four and a half years after the assassination of JFK, there is no way you can tell me that something very sinister wasn't at play in America. I didn't know what it was or where it came from. I only knew that some very dark forces had taken hold in our country. Those who pushed things too far got taken out. Nowadays, progressive envelope-pushers get silenced with character assassination, which seems to be almost as effective.

Up to that point in my life, in 1968, there was still a good chance that I could have gone home to Scarsdale after college to take a job with my dad, with the full understanding that someday I would take over his business and spend the rest of my life as a respectable suburbanite enjoying the pleasures and comforts of the leafy suburbs of metropolitan New York. By the time I woke up from the living nightmare of Bobby Kennedy's assassination, the trajectory of my life had changed.

• • •

I didn't go to Chicago for the Democratic National Convention, but I had a lot of friends who did, who came back to St. Louis with their heads bashed in by the cops. If the feeling of the counterculture had been an abstraction to me before—kind of like a fun thing to do—it became dead serious after the Kennedy killing and the police riot in Chicago.

That summer, like the previous one, I worked for my father in his apparel business, Zimco Industries. I made up swatch cards for his sales force to present as fabric samples to their customers. I packed raincoats into boxes in the distribution center. I drove a truck, picking up finished product from his factories in Connecticut. All the while the Bobby Kennedy assassination lurked in my mind and I watched live TV of the police riots in Chicago.

I voiced my outrage over what was going on to my parents, and I guess the best way to characterize their reaction was that they didn't want to hear about it. They pushed back on my outrage, especially my father. As the conversations grew more unpleasant, I knew better than to push the issue. We each knew what the other believed, and that our beliefs didn't mesh. The main thing was, we were family, and that was more important than politics. I dropped the subject, did my work over the summer, and couldn't wait to get back to St. Louis. I'm pretty sure they both voted for Nixon over Humphrey in the 1968 presidential election. I don't really know.

My junior year, opposing the Vietnam War became the moral issue of our time. Nothing else going on in any of our lives was more important than calling attention to and voicing our opposition to the American war machine. Forget about going to class. A teach-in did more to deepen our understanding about one of the worst foreign policy atrocities in American history. We didn't just challenge the war; we challenged each other: to do more to stop it, to participate less in the social inertia that allowed Vietnam to happen. Everything in American society that supported—or ignored— what was going on in Southeast Asia became an object of our ire.

In my senior year, in November 1969, me and three other college buddies jumped into a Volkswagen bug and headed to Washington, DC, for the Vietnam War Moratorium, a march that drew at least a million people to protest the Southeast Asian genocide. By the time we crossed the bridge into the nation's capital, the crowd had grown massive and, in some places, rowdy. As soon as we could, we parked our car and jumped into the fray. Cops on horseback lurched into the crowd at some points along the march, giving me a taste of tear gas. We didn't have a place to stay, but we hooked up with some locals and they gave us all the floorspace we needed to roll out our sleeping bags. To the same extent that I was traumatized by Bobby Kennedy's assassination, I was heartened by the camaraderie of the protest and its sense of common purpose. It was a feeling of shared goals and values that stuck with me forever.

Back on campus during spring semester, some of the more intemperate forces on our side burned down the Army ROTC building. In late April, Nixon ordered the invasion of Cambodia. Up at Kent State, four student protesters who expressed their disagreement with Nixon's escalation of the war were shot dead by the Ohio National Guard, setting off a nationwide uproar at college campuses across the country. At Wash U., another post–Kent State arson fire gutted the Air Force ROTC building. Fortunately, no one was hurt—until afterwards, when hundreds of peaceful protesters who had nothing to do with the fire bombings gathered for a demonstration at the Francis Field House. I remember watching from a hillside outside our fraternity house when two school buses pulled up packed with maybe fifty county sheriffs wearing riot gear. They filed out of the vehicles and waded into the crowd with their clubs, swinging on anybody they could reach, grabbing bodies and dragging them to the buses.

I got more actively involved the same spring when I took my place in a crowd of thousands in the campus quadrangle to occupy the administration building. There must have been five hundred cops who formed a line around us while our student body president, Ben Zaricor, stood on the steps of the administration building. Ben shouted through a bullhorn, telling us to remain calm and peaceful, but also to press forward with our task. We did occupy the building, peacefully. We made our point, and a couple of hours later, we left, and nobody got hurt. The leadership that Ben showed at that moment is a picture that has been ingrained in my memory forever. For me, it was one of the defining moments of the entire era, at Wash U. and around the country. One of the great fortunes of my life was to later become good and close friends with Ben and his family. Maybe thirty years later, when our families took a vacation together, Ben and I stepped outside together for a couple of puffs on a joint, and Ben asked me if I had any heroes.

"Yeah," I told him. "You."

Ben had a friend at Wash U. who got a very bum rap that upended his life in ways that none of us could imagine. The friend's name was Howard Mechanic, and like thousands of us at Wash U. and across the country, he was outraged by the Kent State killings. At the demonstration at the Air Force ROTC building, he was falsely accused and unjustly convicted of throwing a cherry bomb at the firefighters who responded to the fire. Facing a five-year term in federal prison, Howard skipped bail and went on the lam. He wound up in Scottsdale, Arizona, where he changed his name, built a new life, and in 2000—his sense of community involvement getting the better of his fugitive status—he ran for a city council seat. During the campaign, a newspaper reporter outed him. Howard was rearrested, charged under a fugitive statute, and sentenced to more prison time beyond the five-year term that he had avoided for nearly three decades.

When news outlets picked up the story across the country, Ben contacted me and said we had to do something about it. We did. We got ahold of William H. Danforth, the Wash U. chancellor from 1971 to 1995, and he wrote a letter to President Bill Clinton. On his last day in office, Clinton pardoned Howard.

• • •

Amid the fun, excitement, protests, and disillusionments of college, I did manage to maintain enough of a presence in class to graduate in four years. My senior year, we didn't even have to take any finals. Thanks to the ROTC disturbances and the ongoing nationwide campus revolts over the Kent State massacre, the administration canceled them.

To show our appreciation, we put on a little demonstration at our graduation ceremony. About half the class stood up during the speechifying and turned our backs on the stage. I don't know about everybody else, but my parents didn't appreciate our protest. They were on one side and we were on the other and there was no reconciling the oppositions.

Still, I accepted my Bachelor of Arts degree in economics, which was kind of a joke. I carried almost nothing from my study of traditional economic theory into the practice of my working life where I built a $2.5 billion company. I learned more from reading I did on my own time, Herman Hesse and others. From watching Ben Zaricor inspire the masses. From laughing at Harvey Krasilovsky riding his chopper up the stairs. From the protests, the teach-ins, the frat parties, and the social life that helped me along toward my goal of becoming a fully functioning adult male.

The academic program, at least at that stage of my life, didn't resonate with me. I used to give speeches that made fun of what I learned in college. My standard line was that almost everything they teach you in college is wrong, and in no subject was that opinion truer than in economics. Take the classic definition from Paul Samuelson in the Econ 101 textbook: "Economics is the study of how people and society choose, with or without the use of money, to employ scarce productive resources which could have alternative uses, to produce various commodities over time and distribute them for consumption now and in the future among various persons and groups of society." I guess that's one way of looking at it, if you're talking about gold and oil. But what if the resource is information? Or people?

From the get-go, I thought that this presentation of traditional economic theory was a crock. I guess you could say it was just all too rational, when world dynamics and interrelationships can be very irrational, even emotional. Feeling, if you ask me, has just as much a place in decision-making as fact. But in traditional American economic theory, emotion is not a factor. Applying it to something that I knew a little bit about—like my father's company—I believed that the entire concept of traditional Milton Friedman, University of Chicago–style economic theory, at least the way it was being taught at the college level in the United States of America, was completely wrong.

According to Friedman, people and their labor weren't even classified as a scarce resource. They were just something to be used by the shareholder class at will. These guys peddled supply-and-demand as if it were religion. I questioned then, and I question now, the tendency to think of people who work for wages as anything more than abstractions. Milton Friedman didn't care if workers gained any fulfillment from their labor, or if consumers got the best value, or if the public had to suffer environmental consequences.

It was unthinkable under traditional economic theory for a business owner or entrepreneur to seek their employees' input, to work to unleash their creative energy and constantly improve the process of production. Same with customers. Same with communities. As a college student who knew somewhere deep down that he might be going into business for himself one day, I already knew that some of these concepts just didn't match with reality.

I was never a socialist, even during my college days when many of the people in the circles of radicalism that I frequented were diehard Marxists. I have always been a capitalist in theory, and, of course, later in practice. I've always thought that Adam Smith got it right. The problem, however, is that a lot of his adherents screwed it up.

There had been some writing on "stakeholder theory" as early as 1963, although I don't recall being exposed to it when I was in college. Still, the wheels of my brain whirled. I knew there had to be something different. A kernel had been planted in my mind at Washington University in St. Louis, in my learning in and outside of the classroom, and in the brains of thousands of other entrepreneurs at other institutions of free and forward thinking. We wanted something more humane. More egalitarian. More environmentally conscious.

At the time, the idea of hippies like myself questioning the thinking of Milton Friedman was nothing less than absurd. Our hair was too long, our ideas too unconventional, and many of us dreamt them up while sitting in the lotus position or after smoking a doobie.

We had nothing to contribute, nothing to teach the kings of capitalism. Until we did.

$$\dashv 3 \vdash$$

Transitions

After graduation in the spring of 1970, I had only one thing on my mind: beating the draft. Once I lost my student deferment, I needed to pull as high a number as possible in the draft lottery activated by the Nixon Administration in 1969 to more efficiently decide who qualified to go off and get killed in Vietnam. Something in the 200s would have been fine.

No such luck, with a 35, I think, which pretty much guaranteed me a trip to the jungle with my new 1-A draft status. The Army didn't waste any time. They sent me my draft notice within a month of my graduation.

I had done some volunteer work as a draft counselor back at Wash U., and now it was time to put my knowledge to work for myself. One trick that I remember was for the prospective inductee to check off every illness or disease that is listed on the questionnaire. They name it, you had it—cancer, pneumonia, broken bones, heart palpitations, all of them. I think the list was forty-eight diseases long.

Ticketed for a trip to the induction center, I'd already planned my escape ahead of taking the physical, in case the Army doctors found me to be a picture of health. Canada loomed only 340 miles from my parents' home in Scarsdale, where I hung out while I sweated out my unwanted military career. A little more than ten thousand American men crossed the St. Lawrence River and other stretches of the northern border to beat the draft during the Vietnam War years. I fully prepared to add myself to that number, with the full support of my parents, who didn't want to see their oldest son sent off into the dangers of war.

But I caught a very big break. Even as he expanded the war into Cambodia, Nixon's so-called "Vietnamization" of the conflict turned more of the duties of the war over to our South Vietnamese hosts, reducing the number of US troops over there to 334,600. That was down from 1968's peak level of 536,000, on its way to a cancellation of the draft in 1973. Had I graduated two years earlier, I'd have been dead meat. By 1970, I had a puncher's chance of getting out of the draft by using the same tricks that in 1968 would have gotten me nowhere.

I duly reported to the Whitehall Street Induction Center at Battery Park, the same one that Arlo Guthrie popularized in the movie *Alice's Restaurant*. It seemed like I knew about a quarter of the people there, from Scarsdale, and the other 75 percent seemed to be mostly college grads, like me, stressing out about the possibility that our lives were about to get turned inside out by our country's fucked-up foreign policy. During the mental exam, I was in a room with a couple hundred other guys. Most of them were at least semi-intelligent, and we were all talking to each other about how to get out of this shit, which really pissed off the guards. They were telling us to shut up, and we shot back, "So what are you going to do if we don't, send us to Vietnam?" The problem was that, yeah, that was exactly what they planned to do.

Anyway, at the end of the day, I sat down for my physical, administered by a young medical intern whose name I wish I could remember. He asked about the typhoid fever I'd checked off on my list of illnesses. I gave him some kind of bullshit answer, and he nodded his head, and then he noticed that I listed skin cancer as another affliction that would prevent me from serving.

"Let's see it," he said, and I pointed out to him a mole on my arm, to which he responded, "It looks more like a mole to me."

A little bit more of this and the intern by now probably had a good idea about what was going on—I'm sure he'd seen it several hundred times before. As he continued to look over my paperwork, something caught his eye.

"I see you've just graduated from Washington University," he said.

I nodded sullenly in confirmation, not prepared in the slightest for what came next.

"That's where I went to medical school," he told me.

I should have told him about my twisted testicle, to see whether he was one of the medical students who watched my surgery in the hospital amphitheater. It would have been the one real condition that came up in our meeting. I didn't press my luck. Instead, I only told him that I sure loved our alma mater and that my game plan was to head back to St. Louis if the Army didn't press me into the imperialist war on the indigenous peoples of Southeast Asia. I told him I was still paying rent on my apartment near the school and that I had a substitute teaching gig lined up in St. Louis for the fall.

"Mr. Zimmer," the doctor said, "you don't want to be in the Army, do you?"

"No sir," I told him. "I don't."

"Very well," he said. "All I can tell you for now is that your medical test results are inconclusive. We're going to have to retest you in six months. Until then, we're going to make you 1-Y."

As far as I was concerned, this was like getting a phone call from the governor right before they dropped the pill. I stifled my urge to whoop it up. The 1-Y classification meant that they'd only call my number in case of war or national emergency. I guess that tells you all you need to know about what US Army doctors thought about Vietnam—it wasn't even a war. And it certainly wasn't a national emergency.

For me, it meant it was time to party, and the very first thing I did once I received this act of mercy was to drive straight from the induction center in lower Manhattan to the beaches of Key West, Florida. And I mean straight down. I never even went home to Scarsdale. I'd already packed my Karmann Ghia and said my goodbyes to my mother and father. I told them that depending on the outcome of physical, I'd be taking off for either Canada or the furthest southern point in the continental United States.

I lived it up for two weeks in Key West—stoned on hash, mostly. I also indulged daily in the best key lime pie in the world, before I headed back to St. Louis.

I never heard from the Selective Service again.

• • •

Like I told the doctor at the induction center, I'd lined up a job after graduation as a substitute teacher at University City High School, located just two miles from the Wash U. campus. My senior year, I'd moved into a $140-a-month, four-bedroom walkup with three other guys. It was located about halfway between the high school and the college, in kind of a tough, racially mixed area. Me and my roomies each contributed $35 a month for rent, which I covered with the $40 a week I made for my two days of imparting the knowledge of English, math, science, and history to the scholars of University City High.

I ate cheap—pizza, mostly—and had no problem making ends meet. For the first time in my life, I actually supported myself.

Why teaching? It's not like I had a burning passion for the profession. As much as I respected what teachers do, I never saw myself spending the rest of my life in a classroom or lecture hall behind a podium. But I really wanted to stay in St. Louis, which I liked, and where I was comfortable. For now, in my first year out of college, the part-time teaching thing seemed perfect, a convenient placeholder kind of a job in which I could tread water while I figured out my future. If I liked it, maybe I'd even go back and get my credentials.

Young kid that I was, I got a few sideways looks from the full-time high school faculty and administrators, who didn't know what to make of the long, bushy hair and the beard that I had recently grown. If they did have any suspicions about me, they were well-warranted. About half the student body at UCHS was Black, and the year I taught there I endorsed the demand of the campus Black Students Union for the school to create a Black studies program. My support of the BSU did not sit well with some of the older, white teachers, who had been raised with southern sensibilities on the issue of race. To be honest, the kids had grown a little testy. The previous academic year, they boycotted classes for a week, did a little rioting, and even set off an arson fire. I couldn't blame them for being mad and demanding change. Segregation had remained a serious issue on the campus, where white students tracked for college while Blacks were being ticketed for low-wage work, or maybe even prison. Administrators enforced one disciplinary code for the white kids and another harsher one for the Black kids.

Rioting broke out again on campus in the year I taught there, and the administration sought to cool it down by giving everybody the rest of the day off. As I walked to the parking lot, I noticed a bunch of kids hiding behind the bushes and trees near the faculty parking lot and throwing rocks at the teachers' cars when they drove out. Then, here comes the hippie teacher with the long hair and the beard, the guy who understood and supported their cause, who treated them the same as anybody else in class, who gave everybody the same shot, even if he was a lowly substitute. I made it out to my orange Karmann Ghia convertible and headed toward the exit of the parking lot, not knowing what to expect from the bombardiers. But as I looked at the students, I felt pretty sure that I didn't have a whole lot to worry about. Since those days when I picked up poor, blind, mostly Black people in Yonkers and drove them up to the Berkshire Mountains, I'd become very sensitive to racism, as sensitive as a young white man in 1970s America could be. I don't know for sure, but I think the kids felt that they had a coconspirator in their cause with the freaky-looking hippie out of Wash U.

The only thing I do know is that when I got into my car and drove out of that parking lot, the rock shower subsided, and I drove off in peace.

• • •

Outside of those two days a week substitute teaching, I hoped to fill in the other three days leading a discussion group for a pass-fail class that I had proposed under a Wash U. program that had students and the recently graduated create their own curricula. The title of the course, to be taught by G. Zimmer, was "Siddhartha and the Moody Blues."

The idea was to yoke together one of my all-time favorite books, *Siddhartha*, by one of my all-time favorite authors, Herman Hesse, and one of my all-time favorite albums, *Question of Balance*, recorded the previous year by one of my all-time favorite bands, the Moody Blues.

Hesse, I got into him in college, along with other writers such as Robert E. Heinlein (*Stranger in a Strange Land*), Isaac Asimov (the Foundation trilogy), and R. D. Laing (*The Politics of Experience*). I was one econ major who liked these writers a hell of a lot more than Paul Samuelson, or the man up in Chicago, Milton Friedman. These writers opened me up to new ways of understanding the universe and how to act within it.

Siddhartha, of course, is the classic story of the young man in search of himself. The book evoked an emotional response out of me like nothing I'd ever read. Like, how many times in your life do you finish reading a book and then break out into tears? It had been the perfect book at the perfect time, with its account of an imperfect world where nothing is all good or all bad, filled with physical realities that we need to accept and love, and where everything is only a semblance of its true form.

The book made me realize I was on a path. A year out of college, I wanted to pass along the wisdom of *Siddhartha* to all the other Siddharthas who were coming down the line. What better way, I thought, than to ratchet the ageless wonder of the book to this spectacular Moody Blues album?

Same as I worked through Herman Hesse, I pretty much went to every Moody Blues concert within a hundred miles of where I was living, up to the present day. Sometimes, I'd go see them even if they were three hundred miles away.

The way I saw it, Siddhartha set out on his path the same way that the Moody Blues kicked off *Question of Balance* on the first cut of the album: with a question. "Question" happens to be the name of the first song on the album, and it starts like this:

> *Why do we never get an answer*
> *When we're knocking at the door*
> *With a thousand million questions*
> *About hate and death and war?*

It seemed to me that those same words could have been written by Herman Hesse. Same with the final song, "The Balance," which goes,

> *And he thought of those he angered*
> *For he was not a violent man*
> *And he thought of those he hurt*
> *For he was not a cruel man*
> *And he thought of those he frightened*
> *For he was not an evil man*
> *And he understood.*
> *He understood himself.*

The parallels seemed pretty clear to me—Siddhartha's journey into self-awareness on the path to enlightenment, and the Moody Blues' musical interpretation of the journey of their own self-discovery. I never met anybody in the band, but somehow, in my reading of the book and my listening to the album, I just felt that the group had the book in mind when it produced the album.

I scratched out a single, short paragraph of intent—not exactly a class outline, I must confess—and I let it fly, straight from the heart. You start with Siddhartha as a book of self-awareness, follow Siddhartha through assorted stages of life and the lessons he learns from them, until he himself becomes a buddha; the later discovery that he fathered a son, and his realization that he has to let go as a father and let the boy pursue his own path toward enlightenment. Then, a soundtrack.

Unfortunately for my academic career, the gatekeepers didn't see the connections that were so clear to me. They rejected my idea for the class. "Frivolous" is the word I got from the Wash U. faculty.

Who knows? Had they allowed me to pursue it, maybe I would have become a great professor, and nobody would have been able to buy name-brand suits for $100 less than what the competitors of the Men's Wearhouse charged. Oh, well. I got over it soon enough, pretty much by the end of my first and only year as a substitute teacher, when I got a phone call from my father.

Like Siddhartha, I was about to begin my own journey, also through Asia.

• • •

The kids at University City High dug me, and I dug them, but we had to cut it off when my dad asked me if I wanted to accompany him on what was supposed to be a six-week business trip in the fall of 1971, to Japan, Singapore, Hong Kong, Taiwan, and Malaysia.

"Of course," was my answer. There was no doubt in my mind. Who wouldn't want to take off on an all-expenses-paid trip to witness the mysteries of the exotic Far East? Maybe I'd learn something. Besides, I didn't have a whole lot going on in my life right then—just the part-time teaching job. I was, to tell the truth, pretty directionless. A shake-up seemed in order.

My father had stepped up his action over the years, selling lines of clothing he manufactured at factories in Norwalk, Bridgeport, and Stamford. As he got bigger and more successful, he found that he could save substantial sums by moving his manufacturing operations from Connecticut to Asia, where they make the same kind of clothing for a hell of a lot less money.

My dad never specifically told me why he wanted me to tag along. But I think my father had an agenda in wanting me to come along on the trip, and I think it was me.

He'd grown more than a little concerned about my apparent lack of ambition after I graduated from college, about the lack of direction in my life, about my long hair, about my affinity for hippie culture, and about me spinning my wheels on a part-time job halfway across the country in a field in which I didn't have a particular interest. So, he nudged me.

Give my dad credit. It's not like he yelled and screamed and told me he was tired of me wasting my early adulthood. He played it subtle. He didn't tell me about the attractions of the apparel industry. He wanted to *show* me.

More accurately, he put me in position to see it for myself.

These Asian businesses, he told me, they had this thing about first sons following their fathers into their lines of work, how it represented the pinnacle of a man's success, and how they'd get a major kick seeing this American guy who brought his kid along on the trip.

Only there was a little hitch before we took off.

We were supposed to leave on a Sunday morning, in November, but the Friday before our scheduled departure, my father came home from his office in Manhattan and told me that something had come up with the business. He didn't tell me what. He just told me that he couldn't make the trip.

"But you're still going," he said. "On your own."

I didn't quite know what to think about this turn of events, other than that he may have lost his mind, sending me off into worlds I knew nothing about, and in a role for which I was not at all prepared.

"You're sure about this?" I asked him.

"I told you," he responded. "They love number-one sons over there. You're going to represent me. They'll love it."

"All right," I said. "But you know I know nothing about this."

"You'll learn," my father said.

He was right—it wasn't rocket science. The garment industry kept it pretty simple. You show the manufacturers what you want, and they make it for you. How hard is that? That's what my father told me. And he was right.

He and my mother drove me to John F. Kennedy International Airport on the appointed Sunday morning for the flight on Pan Am One to Tokyo. My mother sobbed at the gate for her boy, who was going halfway around the world on his own, at a time when the other side of the world seemed a lot farther away. My father reaffirmed, to her and to me, that everything would be all right.

On the flight over, the manipulations of my father came into focus, at least in my own mind. He'd planned this out, to make me think he'd be coming along on the trip, only to back out at almost the last second. It was a setup, a test. What better way to expose anybody to anything than to throw them into the water without a life jacket to see if they'd sink or swim?

Maybe I wasn't worried about my future, but I know he sure was. He thought I'd drifted into a permanent stonerville, despite the potential that I guess he saw in me. I like to think he saw some talent here that he needed to prod to the fore.

Whatever his plot, there I was in November of 1971, just eighteen months out of college, sitting by myself on an airplane over the Pacific Ocean. I was a little nervous, but I liked the idea of the adventure. It excited the hell out of me, really, just being able to visit some of the most dynamic cities in the world, and not under the cover of a tourist, but as an international businessman, out to make a deal for his father. I'd never before envisioned myself in this kind of role.

In another respect, this move by my father drew me closer to him than ever before, into a relationship that only deepened in love and understanding for the remaining forty-six years of his life, until he died in 2017 at the age of ninety-three.

I mean, I knew a little about his life's work, having played in the clothes racks at Robert Hall and worked for him at Zimco during my college summers. But to be trusted like that, by a man you'd held in the utmost esteem for your entire life, a war hero, a successful businessman, a father who didn't judge you according to the standards of his generation. War hero, hell. He was my hero, and now here he was, treating me like a man. An equal. A partner.

It was the least I could do, to represent him on this trip. Besides, he was paying me $300 a week. Quite a bit more than what I was making as a $20-a-day, twice-a-week substitute teacher in St. Louis.

• • •

When I got to Tokyo to catch my connecting flight to Osaka, I lugged two huge sample bags stuffed with suits, sport coats, and snorkel jackets through the airport to catch my connecting flight. I damn near missed the flight, carrying all that stuff, not to mention my own luggage. Then, when I got on the airplane, still in a frenzy, the flight attendant brought me and all the other passengers on the flight a cup of hot tea. I immediately and accidentally spilled mine into the lap of the Japanese guy in the next seat. You know what? He was so polite, he didn't even flinch.

For six weeks, I lived out of a suitcase from hotel to hotel, in the various Asian mega-towns. I'd wake up at 6 AM and go to the hotel restaurant to drink coffee and eat breakfast and prepare for the day's meetings. Once

I'd made all the contacts I needed to make, I moved to Hong Kong and rented an apartment on the Kowloon Peninsula for the next four and a half months, flying from here to there to meet with the factory owners.

My head still full of *Siddhartha*, I took it all in as just another step on a young man's journey. It probably would have been nice if I'd known what I was doing.

It was true that everywhere I went, I got along pretty well as my father's number-one son, and they helped me muddle my way through a presentation of the garment designs I had brought overseas for my father. At the same time, I gathered fabric swatches and samples of their work that I sent back to my dad to touch and feel. These days, they do it all by FedEx.

My main memory of Japan was being wined and dined by the trading companies that wanted my father's business. I'd meet with them during the day and present the fabrics and types of apparel—snorkel jackets, mostly— that we wanted produced under my father's brand. By night, I found out they weren't kidding about them taking care of the number-one son. They took me to these expensive steak joints that I still think might be the best in the world, certainly the best I've ever patronized. I couldn't believe it—these companies had *vice presidents* whose only job was to show their clients the town, even if the road rep like me was only twenty-three and didn't have a clue. It was interesting for a hippie at heart, watching how international business got done, much of it lubricated with the pouring of sake.

I liked the crash course I received in garment manufacturing during my four months–plus in Hong Kong, even if I felt isolated in Kowloon, where the locals literally walled themselves off from foreign visitors such as myself. It was just as well, I guess. Unable to make any friends, I walled myself off, too, and I engaged in the study of my father's industry—what soon enough would be my own industry—between visits to manufacturing centers there and in Taipei, Kuala Lumpur, and Singapore.

Having graduated with only the vague idea of wanting to go into business, it was probably right about then, during the Hong Kong stay, that I took the unconscious turn toward being a men's clothing merchant. From his side of the pond, my father had almost no choice but to deal with the overseas manufacturers who could make the same kind of coat in Hong Kong for a third of what it cost him at his three factories in Connecticut. I also came to learn, sorry to say, that the quality of the Hong Kong cut was way better than what they turned out in the States.

On my return to New York, I tried to make the case with my father on behalf of domestic production. I'd come to learn overseas that much of the time, you didn't really know who you were dealing with and you could be setting yourself up to get royally screwed. I mostly interacted with limited-liability trading companies that had separated themselves from the production and distribution processes and basically gave you a shrug if somehow your shipment got lost or misdirected during the long trip by sea to New York or Los Angeles. I argued to my dad that when you factored in the time it took to get the finished products over here, the uncertainty of delivery, and the lack of accountability under the rule of law as practiced in some parts of the world, it made more sense to just keep making the stuff in Stamford or Bridgeport. It's a topic he just didn't want to discuss with me, in a debate that has long since been settled, to the point where garment manufacturing is something that America barely does anymore. In 1960, domestic companies manufactured 95 percent of the clothes that Americans bought. By the time I took my Asia trip, the figure had fallen to 75 percent. Today, it's 2 percent.

I'm not exactly proud of the fact that at the Men's Wearhouse, we went along with the trend. At first, we bought and sold American-made apparel almost exclusively. As we got bigger, we couldn't ignore the better deals that Asian companies offered. By the time I left, we had opened factories in a couple dozen countries around the world and ran them out of an office in New York.

A little footnote to my Asia trip: In the end, it all came to nothing—and everything. My father didn't make a single deal with any of the manufacturers I visited. My guess is that he never intended to, that it was all part of his plan to lure me into becoming a merchant.

• • •

While the seeds of my future germinated, I found myself pretty much back where I started when I returned from Hong Kong—still young, still idealistic, not terribly directed, but for the first time in my life, qualified to vote for a president of the United States, and knowing exactly who I wanted to win.

Talk about a no-brainer for the soul of a hippie—I viewed South Dakota Senator George McGovern as the candidate in 1972 who most reflected the legacy of the assassinated Bobby Kennedy. Besides his liberal politics and antiwar stance, which mirrored my own worldview, I liked the fact that McGovern was a B-24 bomber pilot during World War II— the same aircraft that my father had navigated. McGovern flew thirty-four missions out of Italy, which I knew took some kind of balls.

Back in the States, I'd shut it down in St. Louis, and I sure didn't want to hang around Scarsdale, so I packed up the Karmann Ghia and headed to Chicago, to go to work as a volunteer grassroots fundraiser for McGovern. Anxious to get back into the real world, which in my mind meant anyplace other than Scarsdale, I took up a frat brother on his offer to stay at his place in Chicago, which seemed to be overpopulated with flight attendants. It was a very cool pad in a thirty-story tower with a great view overlooking the Loop.

And off I went, in the summer of 1972, to knock on doors for McGovern all over Chicago. As McGovern climbed from his early 1-percent poll standing to become the Democratic Party's nominee, it was McGovern all the way, for me—all the way to the landslide shellacking he suffered at the hands of the evil Nixon, the third-worst Electoral College defeat in US history: 520–17.

McGovern's landslide defeat discouraged the hell out of me. From the day of the June 17, 1972, break-in, I knew Watergate was a scandal that went straight to the top of the Nixon White House. It took a couple of years to result in Nixon's forced resignation. I couldn't believe that it didn't bother people the way it did me. Yet the public failed to intuitively grasp Nixon's criminality, and the country returned him to office by a score of forty-nine states to one.

I talked up Watergate door-to-door on my volunteer fundraising excursions through Chicago. This was long before anybody had ever heard of microtargeting. As a canvasser, I was just as likely to be talking to Republicans as Democrats, including big numbers of the latter who would break ranks for Nixon. Nobody I talked to wanted to hear about Watergate, least of all from a smart-assed college kid who didn't even live in Chicago. More than a few of them threatened to kick my ass if I didn't get off their porch.

It all made me feel like Valentine Michael Smith, the human raised on Mars and returned to Earth when discovered by an interplanetary expedition, the hero in the Robert E. Heinlein book that I loved so much, *Stranger in a Strange Land*. Only in my case, the strange land was the country of my birth, in a time of polarization, when predominating tribes didn't take too kindly to freaks who ran outside the herd. Maybe you've seen the sign "Hippies Use Side Door"? It was put up for my benefit.

In the naivete of my youth, I actually thought McGovern had a chance. I think my father had a far more realistic reading on the polls. Before the election, he asked me about my plans once the balloting was done.

I told him I really didn't have anything cooking.

"Okay," he told me, in the days before McGovern got punched in the mouth by about eighteen million votes. "But if you're interested, you should know that my guy down in Texas just quit on me. His sales territory is open, and I was wondering if you might be interested in taking it over."

I told him I couldn't go right away, not with the election hanging in the balance. "Once this thing's over," I said, "I can maybe give it a crack."

"That works," he told me.

The day of the '72 presidential election, my dad flew me down to Dallas to get going on my new job as his sales rep in Texas, Louisiana, and Oklahoma.

The polls were still open when I arrived at the Fairmont Hotel in downtown Dallas, a luxury joint that wasn't a bad place to recover from what was about to become a severe case of political depression while I looked for an apartment.

A bellman helped me up to my room with my bags. As I tipped him, I asked, "What do you think, man? Does McGovern have a chance?" Last thing I remember was the dude walking down the hallway and turning the corner toward the elevators, laughing his ass off.

· · ·

Post-McGovern, I spit the taste of political defeat out of my mouth and dove into my new job as a traveling salesman for my pop. For six months, I basically lived out of my suitcase in sketchy motels. It wasn't exactly pleasant, but my six nomadic months in Asia had prepared me for it, and at the time, there wasn't anywhere else I really needed to be. I drove a new green Buick Electra with a huge trunk that I stuffed with suits, slacks, sport coats, and the like and sold directly from my dad to retailers from New Orleans to Tulsa to El Paso.

I cut my hair and my beard, but one thing I couldn't change was my Jewishness. It was amazing how rednecks could pick up on descendants of

Abraham and vibe them into discomfort. I mean, I don't recall any blatant
anti-Semitism, and I never felt physically threatened. Nobody burned a cross
in front of my Dallas apartment. It's just that for the first time in my life, I
felt like I stood out in an ethnic sort of way, and it made me uncomfortable.
I really had become the stranger in a strange land—me, in Texas, in 1973.
Maybe it was more about me than them, me making assumptions about
where they were from and concluding they hated me because I was a Jew.

The last straw came in Houston, in the beginning of 1973, when I got
into a little dustup with Foley's Department Stores. Foley's was big, like
Macy's-of-the-Southwest big, and I mean right down to the town's Thanksgiving Day parade. With sixteen stores in Houston and nearly seventy
across five states, Foley's for forty-four years attached its name to the city's
Thanksgiving Day parade that was every bit as big in downtown Houston as
Macy's still is in New York City. Charlton Heston once served as the grand
marshal of the Foley's Thanksgiving Day Parade.

Foley's, of course, was one of my father's most important customers,
maybe the most important. It was my job to keep them happy, at almost any
cost, including one that put me at odds with my boss back in New York. It
also led to my decision to create the Men's Wearhouse.

It went down like this:

I'm in Houston in a Foley's store with a Foley's buyer, and I'm showing
him fabric, and I can't remember if I break it out or if this guy specifically
requestes it, but all of a sudden he takes an insane interest in this horrific-
looking swatch of garish, canary-yellow, cheap polyester fabric—Italian
cardboard, I call it. I try to steer the guy away from it, but he is insistent. He
has to have this fabric, in this color, and he orders four hundred sport coats
of the stuff. To be clear: that is four hundred polyester, canary-yellow sport
coats that I know nobody will like, buy, or wear, unless it's for Halloween, or if
they are impersonating bananas on one of those floats in the Foley's Thanksgiving Day Parade. I try to talk him out of it, but he insists on the order.

Anyway, I go ahead and place the order and make the delivery. Sure
enough, the coats don't sell. A few weeks later, the buyer calls me up and
says, "I want you to take them back." I tell him that that's not the way it
works, and that he should know that—he bought them, he owns them.

Then, he hits me with, "Hey, I know your dad owns the company. Why
don't you just call him up and tell him to take them back, as a favor to you.
Tell him if he does, I'll make it up to you guys down the line."

It was a real no-class move on his part, telling me to take the stuff back. That should have told me everything I needed to know.

Then I compound the mistake of selling him the coats in the first place by believing his promise of giving me substantial business in the future. But, he's a Foley's guy, and Foley's is my dad's biggest customer in this part of the country, so I tell him I'll see what I can do.

I call my dad. He blows his stack.

"We just don't do business that way, George," he tells me. "If we did, we wouldn't be in business very long."

I explain to him that this is Foley's, the Macy's of Houston, with a parade to boot, and that if we suck it up on this one, they'll make us good in the long run.

Grudgingly, my dad goes along with the take-back—totally against his gut instinct and the best practices of the clothing merchant that he was. And I go back to Houston to retrieve maybe 350 of these coats that I never wanted to sell in the first place. When I'm down there, the buyer takes me to a warehouse, where he's got these insults to men's fashion hanging on the rack—and the son of a bitch goes down the line and lifts up a bunch of sleeves on the coats to show me that they've all been ripped. Neatly. In about the exact same place.

It looked to me like they'd been slashed, likely with a box cutter, and probably by him.

"Now you've got to take them back," he tells me. "They're damaged."

I hold my tongue. I take back the coats.

"Oh," he tells me. "And I've got some other bad news for you. We're dropping your dad's company as a vendor."

The guy now, in my view, has sunk to pond-scum status.

I call my father, who doesn't take the news well. It precipitates one of the sharper exchanges that has ever come between us. Exchange might be the wrong word. Besides dishing me out a nice heaping plate of "I told you so," I believe he called me "an idiot."

I drive straight home to Dallas, about 263 miles up Interstate 45, and I am steaming, mad as I've ever been in my life, by far. I think every thought you can imagine, about what I'd like to see done to this guy, and to Foley's. Even worse, I've been humiliated in the eyes of the man whom I most respect in the world. I also reflect on how I'm not liking this traveling salesman deal so much, that it's time for me to take charge of my own life.

"What I need to do," I think, "is to be my own boss. To make my own rules as a merchant rather than play by the ones made up by the canary-yellow slasher, or even those of my father.

"I floated through college, moving between the warm, welcoming environments of the fraternity and counterculture. I learned the ins and outs of my father's business all my life. I've been all the way around the world and now all the way around Texas. I've managed to live most of my life around moral and ethical people, and now, after six short months on the road, I finally get why those things are important: because I'll be running into people in this life who deal from the bottom of the deck."

After fantasizing an assortment of violent scenarios for the sport coat slasher, I come up with a more peaceful, if more passive-aggressive, idea.

I'm going to open my own men's clothing store.

⊣ 4 ⊢

The Adult Lemonade Stand

In the early days of the Men's Wearhouse, I interviewed a young man named Steve Cook to fill an assistant manager's opening in one of our Houston stores. Great kid—anxious and ambitious, energetic, smart. I say kid, even though at the time, I think he was older than me.

Ready to go on his first day on the job, Steve showed up at his appointed store even before his nine-o'clock-in-the-morning start time, expecting that the store's manager would be on hand to welcome him to work. The punctual as well as promising newbie noticed upon his arrival, however, that the store was dark—no lights, from the inside out. Starting time rolled past, then 9:30, and then ten o'clock. Still, nobody came around to let him in.

Being a Black man in kind of a white working-class area, and this being Texas, in 1974, Steve grew a little nervous.

Just for the hell of it, he gave the door a little push. Damn if it didn't open.

Steve walked inside, and he called out, "Anybody home?"

No answer.

"Hello?" he called again.

This time he heard a ruffling sound over by the clothes racks on the side of the store, where you could buy a suit for the everyday low price of $44 and a sport coat for $27. Steve went over to the racks, where the clothing fell to just a couple inches off the linoleum floor. He heard some more shuffling amid the swirling suits, before a human figure emerged from beneath the racks, like a bear coming out of hibernation.

But it wasn't a bear, or even a lion, or even a bum who had wandered in off the street. It was just our store manager, Jack Glenn, who popped out from beneath the racks, barefoot and shirtless.

Jack's long brown hair dropped to his bare shoulders—some of our employees thought the dude bore a strong resemblance in physical appearance to Jesus. The only clothes he wore were the pants that he slept in, which matched up with one of those $44 suits.

Snapping to alertness, Jack showed not a spit of self-consciousness about his appearance, or any embarrassment about having spent the night sleeping beneath a clothes rack in the store that he managed. The way Steve Cook told the story, Jack acted as if this was how he greeted every new hire that came through the unlocked door.

"Hey, you must be Steve," Jack said, smiling, with an outstretched hand, after he scrambled to his feet. "I'm the manager, and this is how we roll here. I've been working store hours into today. Take care of business, man, and then you can party!"

Steve told this story a million times over the years at Men's Wearhouse parties and receptions and the like, even at our training sessions, and he always received a huge roar of laughter from his fellow Men's Wearhouse employees. Everybody got it. Everybody intuitively knew where he was coming from, that this was a store that did things a little differently, from the wild and crazy side.

If you worked at the Men's Wearhouse in the seventies, where we started with one store, in Houston, and grew to about a dozen, all in the greater Houston metropolitan area, you'd have heard Steve Cook's story or one like it.

Everybody knew the legend of Jack Glenn, and of other legends in the first years of the start-up that shook the American retail industry.

• • •

If anybody back in my college days had asked me if the plan was to work for my dad, or if I had any thoughts about opening a men's clothing store in Houston, I would have told them, "Absolutely not."

That was before I experienced the disillusionment of Nixon's re-election, before the Incident of the Canary-Yellow Sport Coats gave me an even more profound view of the depths of dishonesty inherent within the human species. By the time I launched the Men's Wearhouse, there was no longer a question about which direction I wanted to go in life. I put every ounce of passion I didn't even know I had into this thing, burning with a competitive fire to show Foley's and America how to do this business right. And not just for me, but for everybody who worked for it, who supplied it, who bought from it, who invested in it. The hippie in me merged with my inner entrepreneur. I'd set my course. I'd found out who I was.

You might think that such a revelation about how low humans could go to make a buck would have sent me into lines of work that were closer to my soul. Like running a zoo, or something. (I love animals.) I would answer that, though it had taken me a few decades to become fully aware of it, the fact was that selling men's clothing was embedded deep down in my soul, literally in my blood after years of exposure to my father's business. Instead of driving me away from the apparel industry, the Foley's experience served as a major motivator for me to make my mark within it.

Who knew that the hippie warrior would plant the flag on the battle-field of men's apparel? There had to be a better way, and I designated myself as the guy who could make the change—even force the change. For seven years, I'd rallied for and supported change in foreign policy and civil rights. Why shouldn't this same impulse apply to merchandising? It dawned on me that a good merchant had the potential to affect minds as much as the most ardent activist or erudite campus academician. The merchant sometimes sees the world as it really is, like I did on the road as a traveling salesman. It was a dirty world out there, and somebody from the merchandising hemisphere needed to help clean it up. I figured, it might as well be somebody who could combine the traits of the alpha male with the ethic of the hippie, a perspective on the world that benefited here and there from a couple puffs off a joint.

By the time I got home to Dallas from Houston, in January 1973, I had the idea of the Men's Wearhouse already worked out in my head.

One thing I knew for sure: I needed to write my own rules—no more working for anybody, not even my dad. And why not in the world of gar-ments? I didn't really know anything else, and felt no calling to a different field. I had some experience in it, overseas and as a traveling salesman. Money? It really didn't matter to me that much, then or now. Even though I've made a few dollars in my day, you'll never find a worse money manager. My first three years at the Men's Wearhouse, I paid myself $600 a month. I drove a green Ford van with the Men's Wearhouse logo on the side and the back stuffed with pipe racks, sport coats, suits, and slacks—it really went over big with women, when I picked them up behind the wheel of some-thing the Hillside Strangler might have driven.

But anyone who has started a business knows it takes much more than something like a fleeting desire for revenge to sustain it. Once the vengeance factor receded, I mainly just wanted to make my mark in the world. The light bulb had gone off. I was ready to roll, to work around the clock, like I'd never been motivated to before in my life. In time, I found the construction and operation of a men's clothing store to be my art, and the Men's Wearhouse became my canvas. I would become the Mozart of the merchant world.

Back home in Dallas, I sprung the idea on my dad: to open my own store, in Houston, selling men's clothing for way less than anybody else in town.

He thought my idea was terrible. I know it sounded odd to him, me being a guy who, up until the trip to Asia, never wore a suit for more than two days in a row in his life. I believe his first words to me when I sprung it on him were something like: "What the fuck?"

"You're the son of a manufacturer in New York," he told me. "Stick with being a road man. You're going to be making $100,000 a year before you know it. It's a good job. And you want to open a fucking store in Houston? That's an entry-level job in our industry, son. You do that, you're going backwards."

I didn't disagree with him. But I did tell him that on a personal level, this living on the road wasn't working for me. I hated sleeping in motels. I couldn't stand the constant motion, the inability to make friends or work on my social life. Mainly, I felt deeply uncomfortable as a Jew roaming the land of the redneck. My whole life, being Jewish was central to who I was. It was a huge part of my parents' stories—my dad, who'd had to hide his Jewishness in a Nazi prisoner of war camp, and my mom, who was the orphaned daughter of a Jewish refugee from Ukraine. Growing up in Scarsdale, joining a Jewish fraternity in college—one of three on the Wash U. campus—I'd always felt surrounded and embraced and comforted by Jewish culture. Out there in Texas, Oklahoma, and Louisiana in the early 1970s, I definitely got a sense that I was on my own, on hostile turf. I got a sense out there, for the first time in my life, that there really was something called anti-Semitism. I was made aware of my "otherness." You know it when you feel it, and I felt it.

Once again, my dad, being the great man that he was, heard me out. From 1,500 miles away, on the phone, I could feel him listening, letting it in, feel him nodding his head, feel him getting it. Feel him feeling me.

"All right," he said. "Can you do me a favor, though? Can you hang in there until I find a guy to replace you?"

"Of course," I said.

For the next seven months, I worked his retailers on my old circuit, until we opened the Men's Wearhouse in August of 1973. Even for three months after that, I stayed on with him, working the road Monday through Thursday and keeping Fridays and weekends free for my new responsibilities at the Men's Wearhouse.

Two jobs, seven days a week; even when I dropped the road work for my father, no off days. And I loved every second of it. Like I've said over and over again about my forty years at the Men's Wearhouse, I feel like I've never worked a day in my life. Another thing I've always said: If you're starting a business, don't get married—unless your wife is doing it with you. Your business becomes your family. I eventually did get married—twice, and I had two families that produced three fantastic children and two lovely grandchildren, not to mention two ex-wives.

Ready to undertake the enterprise, I found myself a bit short on capital. I only had $7,000 saved to contribute to the start-up, which primarily went to pay the first and last month's rent. It should come as no surprise that the first guy I asked for help was my father. He had the clothes, and he spotted me a $100,000 line of credit in the form of a rolling inventory that we leaned on for several years, until we really got our feet on the ground and made our pivot toward success. He believed in me, and his trust paid off hugely for him in the long run, when I gave him a one-third ownership in what became a multibillion-dollar business.

With my father in the fold, I went back to my best college pal, Harry Levy, to see if he wanted in for the same $3,000 that I had invested. Harry had grown up in Texas. He knew Texas. And he was available. He had just graduated and was still up in St. Louis when I asked him in. He was more than happy to quit his job up there and help launch our business. There went another third of the ownership. Harry also had a cousin who lived in Houston and who signed on as our first employee. The three of us moved into the same apartment.

We found a storefront in a strip mall on Westheimer Road in the city of Houston, about ten miles west of downtown, and we put down $4,200 for the first and last on a four-month lease. We called the place Store Number

One. For the next thirty-five years, men walked out of there liking the way they looked.

As for a name, Harry and I had initially wanted to call it "The Apparel Mart." Thankfully, somebody up around Dallas had already taken it. We sat on the courthouse steps in downtown Houston trying to come up with something else.

At first, we were thinking about "The Menswear House." A little editing, and we had it—"the Men's Wearhouse." It sounded good enough to last.

On the day before we opened, my dad dispatched an eighteen-wheeler from a factory in Connecticut filled with rolling coat racks as well as thousands of double-knit sport coats and thousands more double-knit slacks. Nothing else—no shirts, ties, shoes, or belts. Suits? We didn't carry any of those for two more years. We couldn't afford them. What did you expect from a store that didn't even have any ceiling tiles? The exposed industrial light fixtures might be stylish now, but they sure weren't then.

The night before our Saturday opening, we worked until midnight rolling the racks into place, tagging the inventory, and hanging it up on the racks, along with the million other things you have to do on the big day. At midnight, I sent Harry and his cousin home and stayed until 2:30 AM cleaning the place up, until all that was left was a gigantic pile of cellophane that the clothing had been wrapped in. I was so damn tired I just collapsed in the middle of it and fell asleep.

When Harry and his cousin showed up in the morning, there I was—in a suit, behind the counter, drinking a cup of coffee.

It was go time.

Thanks to the ads we'd placed in the Houston papers, bargain hunters by the dozens came on down to Westheimer Road to take advantage of our going-into-business promotion. We put a $25 price tag on the coats and $10 for the pants, and we'd sell you two of each for $69.99. For sure, the "two-plus-two," as we called it, afforded you no break on the price. But it sure got the point across that thirty-five bucks for a sport coat and a pair of slacks was a hell of a value—and even more so when you doubled up. It was our first lesson in the "value of the multiple" that we extended over the years into suits. Man, did it increase our volume.

When our first day was done, we had grossed $3,000, and the three of us thought we would all become millionaires.

We wrote out receipts on a memo pad and kept our copies in a cigar box—cash only. Credit cards? Forget about it. We didn't take them.

• • •

I called our little operation "the adult lemonade stand."

The first weekend, it was just the three of us: me, Harry, and his cousin, David. We didn't just stock and sell clothes. We did everything. We cleaned the toilets. We swept the floors. We washed the windows. We dusted the countertops. We answered the phones. We opened the store. We closed the store.

It took us less than a week to realize we needed help. We conducted our recruitment effort with even less sophistication than what you would expect from little kids running a lemonade stand on a street corner. If they needed to staff up, they might hustle their brothers or sisters or next-door neighbors to take a shift now and then. The three of us? We literally hired our first outside crew right off the street—the first people we saw. Who needed a human resources department?

It was the Thursday after our opening weekend, our fifth day in existence. We worked the store until ten o'clock that night before the three of us got into Harry's car to drive home to the apartment. We stopped at a red light, less than a mile away from the store, at Westheimer and Hillcroft Avenue, right next to another car where three young women about our age also waited for the green. It being a summer night in Houston, we all had our windows rolled down.

I yelled over to them:

"Anybody there want a job?"

The driver looked around to her friends, and they all kind of shrugged their shoulders before the woman behind the wheel asked me in response:

"How much does it pay?"

I told them $5 an hour, or more than triple the going minimum wage of $1.60.

Hell, yes, they were interested. I wrote down our phone number and address and gave them to her. At 9 AM the next morning, when they showed up to 6100 Westheimer suite 136, we doubled our work force and attained gender balance, all at the same time.

The three of them—I wish I could remember their names—they caught on quick. They did everything the same as us three except maybe better. They worked the floor, the register, everything. One thing I really noticed was how well they connected to the men who made up just about all our clientele. For all the days of the Men's Wearhouse, as long as I was around, I tried to keep the sales staff—"wardrobe consultants," we called them— 50-50 men and women. These three women impressed the hell out of me. After they made a sale at the cash register and bagged up the merchandise, they would walk *around* the counter and hand it to the customer, personal and direct. It established this immediate intimacy between us and them, the business and its customers. What a touch!

The next week, all by myself, I put up "the sign."

Being the adult lemonade stand that we were, there was no way we could afford $5,000 for a decent neon sign to place on the roof over the store. So, I hand-painted a fairly thick and very heavy piece of plywood, several feet by several feet, and carried it up a ladder onto the roof. Mind you, we were in a fairly classy little strip mall. Briargrove Plaza today has a couple of decent restaurants, some higher-end fashion stores, and a ski shop (yes, in Houston). And here I was, hauling this piece of wood onto the roof and ratcheting it into a steel-pipe superstructure. You try that today and you're going to get the planning department or somebody on your ass, even in Texas. That day, it was about ninety degrees, humid as hell, the dog days of August. It felt like it was raining up there when I climbed down the ladder to grab this miniature spotlight kind of contraption that we bought and slung it up to the roof. Back down the ladder. Back into the store, and I ran a 100-foot-long extension cord out the front door and up onto the roof, from which it dangled free and easy in the breeze. This was Texas in the early seventies—anything goes. I adjusted the spotlight to make sure it perfectly illuminated the beautifully crafted handmade sign. Forty-eight years later, I still can't believe I got it up there by myself.

Some folks might have called it tacky. Some folks did call it tacky. Me, I called it effective. Finally, you could see from the busy street that some kids had come to town and opened a men's clothing store. I'd never been prouder of myself.

The thrill lasted a week, until Tropical Storm Delia came to town and blew the sign down. Smashed it straight into the hood and windshield of a vehicle parked in front of our store.

We did not qualify for federal disaster relief. Instead, our insurance company had to handle the first claim filed against us—covered under Texas law as the result of an "act of God."

· · ·

Tropical Storm Delia, we could handle. The 1973 oil embargo was tougher. Try opening a business when everybody's worried about having enough money to fill their car up with gas. If you were alive in October 1973, right after we opened our store, you know what I'm talking about. If you weren't, think about spending an hour or more in your car inching toward the gas pump. Last thing you want to do after that mess is buy a sport coat and a pair of slacks.

We made it through that first year, though, thanks to my dad and what amounted to the rolling line of credit in the form of the inventory he provided us.

About a year after our opening, a guy named Richie Goldman walked into the store. He fought out of Hazelton, Pennsylvania, by way of Rutgers University. He was about my age, and what do you know—another Jew! Like me, Richie was new to Houston and committed to making a name for himself in his new town. I took an immediate liking to him, even though he came into the store to sell rather than buy. Long-haired and a natural-born marketer, Richie persuaded me to go for a spot in this Penny Saver–like ad circular that he was hustling. I said sure, and damn if it didn't result in a sales uptick.

Richie worked us regularly for the next year, and we liked the results so much that I asked him, "How would you like to get in on the ground floor of the Men's Wearhouse?" I could use a marketing director, and I figured him perfect for the part. It took about a year for the idea to sink in, for Richie to see that we were doing something right, and that it could be worth his while to hop aboard.

His decision to join in, however, led to another one that was very tough for me to make. The way things worked in those days, the only way I could reel in Richie was to cut him in on the action. This left me with the heart-rending realization that I had to part ways with Harry Levy.

In 1975, when we still stashed our store receipts in a cigar box, we needed sales and marketing help. Harry, to be frank, couldn't work the floor for the life of him, and he didn't have a clue when it came to the ins and outs of mass persuasion. In fact, he was so bad with customers that my father, at a family reunion, pulled me aside and advised me, in exceedingly harsh terms, to get rid of him or risk the whole operation going under.

I didn't want to do it. I didn't like doing it. And I still feel bad about it. But my father was right—Harry, in the infancy of the Men's Wearhouse, had to go.

Only problem was, Harry owned a third of the store.

• • •

Eventually, I had my sit-down with Harry. Without question, it's one of the most difficult conversations I've had in my life. I loved the guy. But there was no way around it. I had to tell him that the moment called for strong sellers. Harry pouted, but he knew I was right. He agreed that it would be in our mutual interest for him to pursue other options. This enabled Richie to come in with his marketing genius, at a cost of $3,000 to buy Harry out. As a sweetener to my frat brother, we threw in a brand-new Lincoln Continental worth $22,000. Harry walked away happy, and he was still happy when we hired him back four years later when he went to work as our chief technology officer. Years ahead of the supply-chain game, Harry built us a point-of-sale computer tracking system that linked our cash registers to our inventory.

As for Richie, we became very close friends, too. We sealed our friendship early on around a big promotion we were about to have, when we realized we didn't have the inventory to pull it off. Richie scrambled to find us a manufacturer up in Dallas who could take care of our shortfall. The night before the promo, we hauled the van five hours up to Dallas, picked up about eight hundred pairs of pants, and turned right around for the five-hour drive back to Houston. While I put the pedal to the metal, Richie went to work in the rear of the van. By the time we got back to the store in time for the promo, he had tagged and sorted every pair.

About a year after Richie came in, we picked up another brain who helped take us to the next level—my brother Jim. He'd just picked up his bachelor's in business from the University of Miami ("The U," in Florida) and had been working on and off through his college years in the outlet stores my dad had opened in Connecticut. I guess he was just as influenced as I was, playing in the coat racks during those Robert Hall trips with my dad. Jimmy came to know the merchandising end of the business as well as anybody, a byproduct of growing up Zimmer. He would later become the head of merchandising for the entire chain. We'd always had a great relationship, going back to our Wiffle ball days, and he was actually a terrific athlete who played varsity baseball and football in high school. It turned out that he bought half of my father's interest in the Men's Wearhouse and cashed out nicely when he retired shortly after the board of directors ran me off.

Richie and I remained partners for twenty-five years, until he retired as a multimillionaire in 2000, thanks to convincing me to make the move that led to the massive success of the Men's Wearhouse: investing 10 percent of our gross revenues in television advertising. It didn't take a whole lot of work on Richie's part. I liked the idea from the start.

To get us rolling on the air, we hired one of the most recognizable faces on Houston television in the 1970s and '80s. It belonged to Harold Gunn, who was well-known at the time as the host of the Houston TV version of *Saturday Night at the Movies*. He'd appeared in a vintage World War II–era Army uniform to present what were mostly war and horror flicks, in a show that they called *Captain Harold's Theater of the Sky*.

At first, we kept the production simple: Harold, jumping out from behind a clothes rack to make his pitch. Later, we got more elaborate. In an ad we ran when we opened a new store in Houston, we closed off one of the busiest freeways in town to film Harold dressed like Charlie Chaplin running after a clothing rack on wheels, which Richie and I held by a wire attached to the camera truck. All this in the middle of a busy Houston workday. I would imagine everybody who got stuck in traffic the day we shut down the freeway didn't much appreciate us. I don't know how we got the permit to pull it off.

A guy jumping out from behind a clothes rack, Charlie Chaplin chasing a rack of clothes—cheesy, maybe. But don't laugh. We ran with Harold Gunn as our front man for the better part of a decade, and our sales skyrocketed.

• • •

By 1975, we came to a major moment of truth for the Men's Wearhouse. We had achieved takeoff. It was time for us to bust out of Store Number One to Store Number Two, and Three, and beyond. It was time to do what any successful business venture does, and that is grow.

We had a tiny issue, however, in that we didn't have any capital. A loan was in order, and we got one for $2 million from the San Felipe National Bank of Houston. It's the first place we went, for the very good reason that it was the closest bank to where I lived.

Its president, Robert B. "Bob" Sale, was a fairly impressive guy, an Oklahoma native and a great athlete who graduated forty-sixth out of a class of 633 cadets from the United States Military Academy Class of 1954 at West Point, New York. Once he finished his commitment with the Army Corps of Engineers, he got his MBA from Harvard and then went on to obtain another degree in banking from Rutgers, before he headed back to the Southwest and started the San Felipe bank. Several years after he loaned us the money, he tried to stop a burglar who broke into his house and wound up taking a bullet that left him paralyzed from the waist down at the age of forty-nine. Confined to a wheelchair for the rest of his life, he spent much of it working with patients and raising money for The Institute for Rehabilitation and Research teaching center in Houston for the University of Texas and Baylor University medical schools.

I didn't quite realize at the time what a great thing it was that Bob gave us that loan. The whole experiment of the Men's Wearhouse might have ended right then and there if he hadn't come through for us.

He believed in us for one reason and one reason only: my personal guarantee. It's all I had, being a twenty-six-year-old with no assets. I guess he also liked my attitude. My confidence. The fact that I knew how to bullshit. When I went in to see him, I acted as if I'd already achieved business success—which I had, at a minor level—and that the big winner out of this transaction was going to be his bank. When I told him that I really needed the money, he told me, "We'll take a look at it, George." I said to him, "No, Bob. We've already spent it."

• • •

Thanks to the loan, we were able to open at least one store a year, to build out the company to a dozen locations by the end of the decade. Thanks to the advertising, we drew plenty of traffic. Thanks to our customers, each of our stores generated an average of $800,000 a year in sales.

Store by store, I did the assembly, going for a décor of pipe-rack stark. It took me a couple of days at each location to ratchet everything into place. We loaded them with inventory, into space so tight the customers had trouble getting around each other to explore the merchandise. The floors were linoleum or concrete, the walls barren except for the block-lettered signs that told you what we sold and for how much.

One of our biggest problems in the early days? Robbery. I can't tell you how many times our stores got held up, it was so often.

Perhaps the most memorable stickup occurred at the hands of one of our own employees. I'll call him Tommy. It was a sad circumstance, because I liked Tommy very much and considered him a good friend. He was Black, and he took me two or three times on romps through the little blues bars and clubs down in the 'hood. Saturday Night Tommy looked like somebody out of a Curtis Mayfield song, with his Superfly brims and colorful polyester double-knit suits. Tommy honestly could not have done a better job impersonating a pimp if he dressed up like one for Halloween—probably because he was, in fact, running a few hookers. Who was I to judge? All I know is, the times I went out on the town with Tommy, we had a blast.

Well, one day Tommy walked into Store Number One—with a pistol in his hand. He pointed it at the cashier and told her to give him all the dough.

"You know, I'm really sorry about this," Tommy told the cashier. "Please tell George I'm *really* sorry about this, and if I didn't have to do it, I wouldn't. But,"—as long as he was at it—"you better give me all the money now. And, by the way, I know you hide a little bit in the back. Go get that, too."

Tommy got caught, and last I heard, he took a plea deal. I believe he did a four-year jolt.

We had another character I'm going to call Jason who was a terrific salesman—one of the best we ever had. He called in once to ask if he could leave work early on a Saturday to go camping. I told him, sure, as soon as you first write us up $2,000 in sales. Come Saturday, he went right to work, got on the phone, and had it nailed by noon. Off he went camping.

An hour later, the FBI came in looking for him, I can't remember for what. We never saw Jason again. Too bad—he was a pretty smart guy who taught us the whole concept of "clienteling," according to which we kept a history of purchases on our best customers. We knew what they bought, what they needed, when they'd be ready to come in again.

Another time, the police arrested one of our store managers for drunken driving. Our guy pleaded guilty to the offense, and his sentence included four weekends in jail. To get him through this difficult time, I chauffeured him to the clink as soon as he finished his shift on Saturday nights. Then I'd pick him up first thing Monday morning to get him back to work. It was a small sacrifice to help out a good employee.

As founder and asset protection specialist of the Men's Wearhouse in its early days, I'd go to any lengths to keep us from getting ripped off. One night I walked into Store Number Two and spotted a sales ticket rung up on a Visa card for a sport coats and two pairs of pants. In those days, our people had to get authorization from the issuing company for all credit card purchases, and it looked like nobody had made the call on this particular transaction. I figured I'd make the call to Visa. The Visa people asked, if it wasn't too much of a hassle, could I please confiscate the card? They informed me that it had been stolen. Nothing I could do about that, it seemed to me, until I noticed that the dumbass suspects had left a clue in their wake: on the counter near the sales ticket, a pack of matches, from a nearby Vagabond Motel.

I gumshoed it over to the motel. I asked the desk clerk if anybody by the name on the credit card had checked in. The clerk gave me the room number. I made my way to the room and knocked on the door. The door opened, and I walked in on my prey—two middle-aged white guys, nondescript, drunk, seemingly not so bright. I told them I owned the Men's Wearhouse, that we were kind of just getting started, and that as a new promotion, I made it a point to meet as many of our first-time buyers as I could and take them out for a drink, to thank them for their business. Surprisingly, the two subjects bought my line. Sure, they said, and we went to a nearby bar, where one of the two—both of whom were now getting deep in their cups—pulled out his wallet and fumbled out a couple of credit cards to buy another round. I told him that I got it, and on my way to the bar I managed to surreptitiously snatch the two credit cards. Then, instead of buying the round, I ducked out of the joint. The next day, the two geniuses called the store about the stolen credit cards. My store manager told them he'd be happy to return the cards if they returned the stolen merchandise. Believe it or not, they did.

Along with thieves and scoundrels, we had to confront another early-years problem in the form of the Texas "blue laws," a byproduct of

Bible Belters who didn't want anybody to do anything on Sundays except pray. Among the restricted activities: buying stuff from men's clothing stores.

Our first weekend in business, we knew we had to get around this abominable breach of the separation between church and enterprise. Remember that $3,000 first Saturday? Well, we drew a goose egg on Day Two, a Sunday, because we couldn't open the damn store. On Monday, our next day back in business, we grossed a big $60. That wasn't going to cut it.

After we opened a couple more stores, we found a loophole that allowed you to remain open if doing so was for a charitable purpose. No problem there—we scored three Salvation Army collection boxes the size of kids' playhouses and placed them inside the three stores. Talk about convenient— same time you're modernizing your wardrobe, you can drop off your old threads for charity! And if you did, we'd give you a discount.

We took the idea to the Texas comptroller's office. They liked it. We were now exempt from the Day of Rest.

• • •

About three years in, it looked like the adult lemonade stand was about to take off. I gave myself a raise, and I had Johnny Carson to thank.

Anybody who ever saw the Godfather of Late Night knew that along with being funny and smart and perfectly in touch with middle-class America, Johnny knew how to dress. He was so good at it that some bright-eye somewhere told Johnny that he ought to start his own clothing line. He did, and it took off, and the day came when a representative from Hart, Schaffner & Marx, the Chicago manufacturer of Johnny Carson Apparel, Inc., made a sales call on little old us.

Up to that point, all we'd been carrying was the stuff we got from my dad. The big boys in Chicago figured our customers might be ready for something a little more swank, so they sent a rep down to pay us a visit. He turned out to be more than your typical circuit-riding suit hustler. We got the big cheese, the senior HS&M vice president, Kenny Hoffman, who later became the company's president and CEO. I don't know what he saw in us, because I didn't see it at that time myself. Maybe he had a crystal ball that told him we would become the largest men's clothing retailer in American history. Otherwise, I can't see how or why the senior vice president of one of the largest clothing manufacturers in the world would fly down from Chicago to Houston to check in with a tiny chain just getting off the ground in Texas.

But there he was, sitting in our closet-sized office at Store Number One, to see if I wanted to buy some Johnny Carson suits.

I'd done my homework, and I knew that Kenny played college basketball (at Loyola–New Orleans, where he averaged 4.6 points a game his senior year against top Division One competition). I asked him if wanted to go out back and take a few shots. We kept a hoop out there for half-court staff pickup games. Some people like to cut their deals on the golf course. In those days, I cut mine—or, at least I cut this one—shooting baskets. We go back there, and the conversation during the shoot-around turned to Foley's, the regional men's retail leader that screwed me not too terribly long ago on the canary-yellow sport coats. Kenny expressed concern about how they might react if he also let me carry the Johnny Carson line in their domain. I told him that I didn't need the Johnny Carson label, so go ahead and sell it to Foley's, no problem. Kenny didn't quite get where I was going with this, but I told him that our adult lemonade stand didn't need no stinkin' labels, that if and when Foley's whined about maintaining exclusivity deals on the Johnny Carson brand, to go ahead and give it to them. Just sell us the suits at 20 percent less, I asked, and we'll sell them without the labels. Furthermore, I told him, it wouldn't bother me if he sold exclusively to Foley's on the first and third quarters, which would give them first shot on the traditionally more lucrative new spring and fall lines. We'd be happy, I said, to take our deliveries off-season, in the second and fourth quarters.

As if our customers cared. As if they couldn't wait until summer or winter to buy. The fact was, they'd do their suit-buying any old time. Thanks to the genius of "clienteling," we were getting to know our customers pretty damn well. We knew that most of them couldn't stand to go shopping in the first place. They wanted in, they wanted out, and they wanted to save a buck. And that's what I told Kenny Hoffman. Sure, the suits wouldn't have the label, but it would still be the same suit. That's all our guys needed to know, even if it said "Men's Wearhouse" on the inside instead of "Johnny Carson."

Kenny liked the sound of it, and off we went. We got the Johnny Carson suits late, and without the label—and we sold them for a hundred dollars less than what they were charging at Foley's, our $199 compared to their $299. Not too long after that, we did it with the Nino Cerruti brand that Hart,

Schaffner & Marx also manufactured. And the next brand, and then the next. Same suit, only no label, unless it belonged to the Men's Wearhouse.

My father, our only supplier before Kenny Hoffman entered our world, didn't particularly like the end of his inventory monopoly on the Men's Wearhouse. Despite the grumble, I knew he'd come around. Maybe he would only be supplying 80 percent of our merchandise instead of 100 percent. Big deal. We were on our way to becoming a billion-dollar company, and he owned a sixth of it.

Foley's? What can I say? This was our biggest move on them yet, toward eventually running them into the ground. Call it the revenge of the canary-yellow sport coats.

• • •

As the seventies came to a close, and as it looked like we had gained a foothold that would guarantee our survival, I thought it was time to decide what the Men's Wearhouse was going to be about, practically and philosophically, in the form of a mission statement, which I scribbled out on the back of a cocktail napkin.

It read, "Our mission at the Men's Wearhouse is to maximize sales, provide value to our customers, and deliver top quality customer service while still having fun and maintaining our values. These values include: nurturing creativity, growing together, admitting to our mistakes, promoting a happy and healthy lifestyle, enhancing a sense of community, and striving toward becoming self-actualized people."

Stakeholder theory had been around for about fifteen years by then, and it would be another fifteen years or so before economists began to flush it out as a concept that competed with Milton Friedman's love for maximizing shareholder value.

As a longtime hippie, a capitalist, and an armchair student of history, I like to date its origins to the writings of Adam Smith, the so-called "Father of Capitalism" and the author of *The Wealth of Nations*. In his less-well-known work *The Theory of Moral Sentiments*, he makes it clear that for capitalism to work, it had to be based on things like integrity, looking out for the weakest among us, and a sense of community, on prudence and empathy. You could say that Adam Smith, then, was not only the theoretical originator of capitalism, but also the idea man behind stakeholder capitalism.

Adam Smith's moral sentiments, however, somehow got lost about the time of the Industrial Revolution.

Once it looked like we had ensured the survival of the Men's Wearhouse, I guess I channeled my understanding of the sentiments of Adam Smith into showing the world in our mission statement how we were going to do business. We were going to make money, all right, but we were going to do it right. We were going to do it like hippies, with the values that we lived by in the sixties.

"I Guarantee It!"

Almost half a life ago, I stepped in front of a camera for the first time in my life to film a television commercial. It would be the first of hundreds of TV spots that would run thousands of times in every major television market in the United States. They would make me almost famous.

My hair was a chestnut brown, and so was the beard, both well-trimmed, betraying nothing of the wild look that I sported in my college days. The three-piece suit fit perfectly across my medium-athletic build. It's been long enough ago that I've forgotten who made it. It looks gray, leaning towards brown—hard to tell, when you look it up on YouTube. I'm pretty sure it's a Nino Cerruti, it looks so damn good—thank you, Kenny Hoffman. Meanwhile, a nice red tie with diagonal white stripes sharpened me up at the collar.

The piece starts out with my face consuming about three-quarters of the camera frame, outlined against a half dozen rectangular sunken ceiling lights shining down from above. I move briskly at an angle between the suit racks—forward, and to the right. I look directly into the camera.

I inform the viewer: "When I opened the first Men's Wearhouse ten years ago, I thought price was everything. I'm George Zimmer, president of the Men's Wearhouse."

With these important facts out of the way, I come to a full stop next to a headless display mannequin dressed in a suit that looks exactly like mine. The camera zooms to the action off to the left, where one of my tailors chalks the sleeve of a customer. A female wardrobe consultant watches from a few steps away.

"As discounting has caught on, I've found that quality and service are just as important as price," my narration continues.

I stood by these words for the next twenty-nine years.

Then, I get to the heart of the matter:

"While others may sell seconds, irregulars, and old merchandise, you'll never find that at the Men's Wearhouse."

We pass the halfway mark of the thirty-second spot, as the camera redirects its gaze toward another customer, wardrobe consultant, and tailor, the saleswoman explaining the finer points of a garment to the gentleman who holds it aloft, the tailor ready to size him up.

Out of nowhere, I come back into the commercial, in a different part of the store, making my way behind a different rack, a wall full of suits to the rear. I proceed at an angle toward the camera, to which I shoot a mysterious sideways glance. Am I about to let the viewer in on a secret of the universe? The key to the afterlife? A discussion on the circularity of time?

"What you will find," I say, "is the same quality clothes sold in the finest stores for at least twenty percent less."

And now, as I look straight into the camera, I drop the hammer. With my right index finger held towards the sky, I emphasize the last and final and most enduring point, the one that I would repeat countless times over nearly three decades, the one that would make my face one of the most recognizable in the history of American television advertising, the slogan that I still receive from strangers on the street more than seven years after departing the Men's Wearhouse:

"I guarantee it!"

• • •

By the time we shot that first commercial, the Men's Wearhouse had broken out of Texas to establish a solid presence in Northern California and the Pacific Northwest. We had about fifty stores pulling in annual sales of a little over a million dollars a year each, with a ridiculously low markup of 40 percent. We were modestly profitable. We'd tested the waters of television advertising and we found that it worked very nicely with our "everyday low pricing" model. We determined, however, that with a little polish on the TV side, we could become enormously profitable.

Harold Gunn, the Houston semi-celebrity who appeared in our first commercials, fit the bill fine for us in the East Texas media market, where everybody knew him and his antics from his late-night TV work and other media ventures. We knew we'd need a different face for Northern California, Seattle, and Portland, and maybe even the rest of the country.

I figured it might as well be mine.

Richie Goldman, our marketing sage, disagreed. He brought in a nationally prominent advertising consultant—at a cost of $100,000—to give us a read. The consultant sided with Richie. But I stuck with my gut. I argued that nothing could be better for the company than for its founder and CEO to be the spokesman, to be perceived as an honest merchant, direct and trustworthy. I knew that if we could make that connection between an owner's integrity and his intense personal interest in the quality of his company, the public would buy it.

I knew our market. I knew our customers. I'd worked the floor long enough to meet hundreds, if not thousands of them. I knew they didn't care about labels or what was "in" that season. They saw a suit as something they had to wear, more like a uniform than a decorative art. They related more to Ralph Kramden than Ralph Lauren. They shopped with common sense, not a fashion sense. They wanted something that was acceptable, available, and, mostly, affordable. We knew that if you were a diva who liked to primp and preen in front of the mirror, you should go buy your suit somewhere else. We were going for the guy who liked the Johnny Carson look, and liked it a lot more if he could get it for a hundred dollars less than what it would cost anywhere else. We sacrificed the label for a good price, which bought us credibility in the eyes of our customers.

I felt that I could deliver this message with more authenticity than anybody.

It helped that I am something of a ham. It's a quality in a person that I appreciated all the way back to when I was a kid going to those Broadway plays on Nana Jessie's comped tickets. I most definitely brushed up on it during my Wash U. years. Every year, my fraternity put on a winter and spring song-and-dance show. One year we did it at the old Kiel Auditorium in St. Louis where the Hawks used to play, before they moved to Atlanta, and thousands of people came to see us. I started out as an understudy in the chorus, before the guy I backed up went out with an ankle injury. When the director told me to get in there—next man up—I told him I couldn't sing or dance, that I'd been totally faking it in rehearsal, that the only reason I got into the gig in the first place was to meet girls.

The director told me, "You'll be fine, George. All you have to remember is to smile when the lights come up. If you're smiling, nobody is going to notice anything else." This simple piece of advice has become my only mantra when it comes to my small corner of what you might call show business.

. . .

In our rehearsal for that first commercial, the plan called for me to finish it off with a line we stole from a Bill Murray film.

Maybe you've seen *Stripes*, in which Murray's character leads his platoon through a funky rifle exhibition drill. The general on the reviewing stand asked if he understood correctly that the unit trained for the exhibition on its own, without the direction of its drill sergeant. To which Murray shouted in reply, "That's the fact, Jack!"

That was supposed to be my tagline in the commercial. Like many other best-laid plans, this one went awry when, for no good reason, my brain rejected "That's the fact, Jack," and substituted "I guarantee it" in its place.

It was a pure ad-lib, and we all have Joe Namath to blame.

Every football fan in America should know about Namath's "guarantee," before Super Bowl III, that the 17.5-point underdog New York Jets would beat the Baltimore Colts. Damn if the Jets and their long-haired, jet-setting quarterback didn't come through, in one of the great sports moments of my favorite decade, the sixties.

I strongly felt going into the filming on that first commercial that the Murray line wouldn't work. Total truth, however: I had no idea I was going to guarantee anything until the three words came out of my mouth, an unconscious recollection of the Namath prediction.

In a flash, I went from feeling awkward and unconvincing to totally comfortable, delivering a promise I knew I had to keep, and one that established an immediate connection between us and the customer.

Less elegant, "Cover the asses of the masses" was the behind-the-scenes ideological underpinning of our business model. That and a guarantee drove our message for nearly three decades.

. . .

We ramped up our advertising at the same time the Men's Wearhouse began to go national, an expansion fueled and framed by bad times and the love of a pretty woman.

When the seventies came to an end, our empire consisted of a dozen stores—ten in Houston, and a couple more over in Beaumont, Texas. We sold about a million dollars a year out of each, on average—not bad.

We'd been thinking for a while about busting out of Houston, testing the waters of the Dallas-Fort Worth area. Then I took a vacation to Northern California, and everything changed. For one thing, I met and fell in love with the woman who would become my wife. I also fell in love with the San Francisco Bay Area. By 1982, I would be married and living in suburban San Leandro.

The thing about founding and owning your own company is you're never really totally on vacation. The wheels are always spinning, even when you're enjoying the blossom of a new love. As long as I was in the NorCal neighborhood, I figured, I might as well sniff around and check out the competition.

On a walk down Market Street, the main commercial drag of San Francisco, I stopped into a Grodin's department store, and then into the rival Roos/Atkins outfit across the street. They were the leading specialty men's stores in San Francisco, winking back and forth at each other across the city's most prominent boulevard. On the same excursion, I thought I'd also stop into the local fortress of one of the biggest dogs on the American retail block—the Macy's in Union Square.

I found that each of these three locations had one huge thing in common—they all charged way too much money for men's wool suits. In San Francisco, nothing retailed cheaper than $300. In Houston, we sold the exact same suits for $199. It seemed pretty clear to me that we stood to make a killing if we expanded into the Bay Area. Hey, nobody loves Dallas more than me. But comparing the numbers, I knew I had to put the metroplex on hold.

California would be the target of our first out-of-Houston expansion.

We made the Almaden Fashion Plaza in San Jose our first location outside Texas, and followed it up with stores in Mountain View, Redwood City, Newark in the East Bay, and Pleasant Hill. In fairly short order, we'd taken over two storefronts on or near Market Street. Talk about location: one of them was on Drumm Street, right across from the Hyatt Regency, in the Financial District. Our landlord, Walter Shorenstein, gave us a great deal. Walter, of course, was a billionaire and a top real estate guy in San Francisco and huge donor to Democratic Party politics. He liked us because his father and grandfather were tailors, or so he told me one night when he had me over to his house for dinner, along with some Democratic luminaries. He knew we took very good care of the tailors we kept in all our stores; he knew that we had to, to back up our promise of a complete fit on a suit within twenty-four hours of purchase.

It was just five years after we had opened stores in these six cities that we went into production on the first "I guarantee it" ad. Surprised by our success, we went all in on TV—locally at first, and then nationally, corresponding with an expansion that did not abate the entire time I held the reins to the Men's Wearhouse empire.

While it was love that drew me to the Bay Area, it was a massive economic recession that forced us out of our comfort zone in Houston.

In 1973, the OPEC oil embargo knocked us for a loop in the rookie season of the Men's Wearhouse. That was nothing compared to nine years later, when a Saudi Arabian–manufactured oil glut, as opposed to a Saudi Arabian–manufactured oil shortage, upended the regional economy of Houston, which expanded or contracted based on the extraction and refinement of Texas crude. Oil prices in East Texas fell by 50 percent in the early 1980s, and the local economy went into the tank.

Houston lost nearly a quarter million jobs. All those big glass towers downtown? Some of them emptied out to less than half full. A couple hundred thousand people lost their homes and left them vacant. Everywhere you looked were half-finished construction projects. Nearly six hundred banks would fail.

Lucky for us, the California stores helped us weather the storm of the Texas depression, which soon folded into the Reagan recession of 1982. California kept us afloat. If not for the success of the Bay Area stores, the Men's Wearhouse likely would have been finished, and I wouldn't have been going on TV to guarantee anything.

There was another thing that we had to ride out: our very survival.

• • •

The original $2 million we borrowed from Bob Sale and the San Felipe National Bank of Houston? We rolled it over to First City National Bank Texas. No real news there, other than that we got a better deal. The First City people, however, got a little bit antsy when the sinkhole of the early-eighties

Houston economy swallowed everything within sucking distance. With the oil glut underway for about two years, they fretted when they reviewed our financials in mid-1983. We tried to tell them that, like most retailers, we didn't really get into rhythm until the holiday season. They said they couldn't wait that long and that we had sixty days to pay off the whole thing.

We hired an accounting consultant named David Edwab to find a path out of this mess, which basically meant finding us another bank to take our loan. While Edwab beat the bushes for a new bank, another issue slammed us upside the head. My father, for all his knowledge of the garment industry, fell $125,000 into debt to one of his suppliers on his factory-outlet business. Eventually, he would liquidate and throw in with the Men's Wearhouse. In the meantime, however, he filed for bankruptcy, which did not please the supplier, Cliftex Co., of New Bedford, Massachusetts, to whom he owed the money.

To get ahead of the problem, I put in a call to Joel Anapol, owner and president of Cliftex, to alert him to my father's impending filing, and that my father was good for the debt. But, to tell the truth, Anapol sounded a little pissed off when I spoke to him on the phone. My father and I agreed to meet with him the next day at his factory in New Bedford to personally guarantee the $125,000. Anapol flew the two of us up from Newark on his private plane. Anapol had a driver whisk us to the Cliftex factory, where a man by the name of Domenick Nicolaci met us outside. Nicolaci, a silent partner in the Cliftex operation, we were told, took me for a little walk.

"You know, George," Mr. Nicolaci told me, putting his arm around my shoulder, "this is a really lovely thing you're doing, taking care of your father's debts." I didn't know exactly what to make of the remark, other than to think that if I hadn't guaranteed the $125,000, the situation had every possibility of becoming exceedingly unpleasant for me and my pop.

The plane ride back to Newark from New Bedford was the most harrowing ninety minutes in the air that I've ever spent in my life. A rolling thunderstorm accompanied our flight on Anapol's little four-seat Cessna. Talk about a white-knuckle job—my dad and me, we took turns gripping our fists around a fifth of scotch that we drained before we hit the tarmac at La Guardia, listening to all these air traffic controllers warning jetliners to watch out for this little Cessna. You couldn't see ten feet out the windows, and the cloud cover didn't break until we were four hundred feet from the runway. I gave us about a 50-50 shot of coming out of it alive.

My guarantee of the $125,000 repayment caused me some big trouble with the people at First City. They said I had violated a loan covenant that prohibited me from guaranteeing any third-party debt, even if it belonged to my own flesh and blood, a war hero who was once shot down and imprisoned by the Third Reich. No doubt about it, there are certain times and certain circumstances in which banks really do suck.

Meanwhile, David Edwab found us a bank that would get us out of the jam with First City. There was one catch, however. They wanted an infusion of $500,000 cash. I checked our bank account. We were $495,000 short.

I went on the hunt for the half million by myself. My other partner, Richie Goldman, told me this was all on me, which did not exactly please me, though I knew Richie always had the best interests of the Men's Wearhouse at heart. I could have diluted his ownership in the company, but chose not to.

My search for the new capital led me across the continent and into Canada, where I met with Wilfred Posluns, cofounder of Dylex, Ltd., the giant retailing and manufacturing conglomerate based in Toronto. I offered Wilfred a 25-percent share of the Men's Wearhouse in exchange for the $500,000. Over the next twenty years, Wilfred's $500,000 investment would have ballooned into a stake worth $500 million.

"George," Wilfred said, "I'm not going to invest the $500,000 now. But you make a profit this year, you can come back again next year, and we'll talk."

All I could say was, "Look, Mr. Posluns, with all due respect, if I make a profit this year, you're not going to be able to buy 25 percent of the company for $500,000." I wasn't trying to be glib. But I was desperate. We had about three weeks to come up with the $500,000, or we'd have to declare bankruptcy.

On the brink of disaster, I played the only card I could—I called my mother.

Despite everything I'd learned and accomplished since I'd gone off to college, wanting mainly to become a fully functioning adult male, I guess I was still something of a mama's boy.

By this time, she was living one town over from Scarsdale, in Hartsdale, New York, taking care of my grandfather, Papa George, who was in his final stage of life. She held his power of attorney, so in effect, I would be borrowing the money from him. Only he wouldn't know it.

I guess she found my coming to her with my hand out slightly per-turbing. I recall her first words to me being something on the order of, "George, I'd like to kill you."

The only collateral I could give her was my word that my brother and I would make this Men's Wearhouse thing work. I also promised her that with our success, we would make sure that our little sister, Laurie, would be taken care of for the rest of her life. Turned out Laurie never really needed us. She married the world-class bluegrass mandolin player and music pro-ducer Rudi Ekstein. Both of them are doing just fine.

Not long after my mother loaned me the money, my grandfather died. A year after that, she got cancer, and she died.

I never doubted that we would pull out of the bank mess. My great remorse, though, is that neither Papa George nor my mother ever got to see how well things worked out thanks to their gift.

• • •

Once we got our financing straightened out with our new banker, and once we decided I'd be the guy to deliver our message, we got back to advertising. I bolstered the personal guarantee that I placed on our product with a prom-ise of "quality, service, and a good price."

We pounded that trifecta into millions of viewers' heads for nearly three decades. I knew enough about advertising to understand that you can only make a message stick with consistency and repetition. For us, it was my guarantee, my later promise that "you're going to like the way you look," and the constant emphasis on quality, service, and a good price.

In one of our early spots entitled "Training Seminar," you saw me giving a little pep talk to a class of salespeople. I took my coat off for the piece, to expose a pair of red suspenders over a white shirt, with the same brown hair and a beard. In that staged training room, I laid it on thick, with words that held the attention of millions of consumers for more than a quarter of a century, words that made up the basic philosophy of the Men's Wearhouse.

"'I guarantee it' means more than just price," I said. "It means service. It's not necessary to sacrifice service or quality to get a good price. At the Men's Wearhouse, you get all three—service, quality, and a good price. And every time you are courteous to somebody, remember that I am back in the office standing on my desk cheering, because that's what retailing is all about."

That was definitely a merchant talking.

By the end of the 1980s, I realized that we were sitting on a gold mine. We'd combined "I guarantee it" with an everyday-low-price model that basically means that your stuff is on sale all the time, except for maybe once a year when you're damn near giving stuff away. We'd tried the everyday-low-price thing earlier, in Houston, but without advertising, and it bombed. With advertising, it was *the* bomb.

We accelerated our growth, into Portland and Seattle. I took a scouting trip to the Pacific Northwest once I got settled in Oakland, and I knew almost immediately we were going to be very successful up there. Those were the two most rip-off cities in America, especially when it came to clothing. Nordstrom, of course, was huge in its hometown of Seattle. They had nice stuff. They also charged a lot, and they were exceptionally easy to undercut. Seattle turned into one of our best markets.

We went back to our original Dallas expansion plan—and extended it into San Antonio and Austin, even San Diego.

We grew to thirteen stores in Northern California, including one in Sacramento where Mike Tyson, who at the time reigned as the heavyweight champion of the world, and his wild-haired promoter, Don King, stopped into one of our stores on an emergency shopping spree. They and their posse had flown into town to pick up some kind of award, but once they landed they discovered that their luggage hadn't made the flight. They had to scramble to look good for their ceremony that night. I don't know why they picked us, but they pulled their two stretch limousines to the front of our store in Loehmann's Plaza, where we outfitted the champ and the rest of his bunch, including Don King, in the latest offerings from Nino Cerruti (without the label, of course).

Tyson represented something of a challenge. According to the tale of the tape from the Larry Holmes fight earlier that year, he stood 5 feet 11½ inches, weighed 215¾ pounds, with a 71-inch reach and a 43-inch chest (45 inches, expanded). More problematic were the 27-inch thighs and his 19¾-inch neck.

It was a good thing we had a team of tailors on the premises, like we did at all our stores. We promised our twenty-four-hour turnaround, but they needed it a lot faster than that. I think we made the alterations in about sixty minutes. Whatever it was, it was pretty damn quick, and Tyson left a huge tip for the tailors.

By the time Tyson got onto us, I would say we had attained a moderate level of success. We were up to about eighty-five stores, each of them pulling in a little over a million a year in sales. Every store we opened killed it.

• • •

As we grew, I decided that we would shape the Men's Wearhouse work-force into the happiest, most productive, and best in our industry. Humane treatment of our employees had been ingrained in the company from the beginning, but as we became more established, it became an explicit initiative. When we started, pretty much the only people who applied were white and male. From the beginning, I recruited outside that box, starting with the three women I literally met on the street. We diversified long before diversity ever became a thing.

Our employees mostly came from lower-middle-class and working-class backgrounds. They'd graduated from high school. They didn't pay a whole lot of attention to politics. They were people who liked to work, who hustled. They were go-getters. They were driven. They liked to smoke and drink, and party—to which I can personally attest. They loved having fun. They wanted their workplace to be fun, and they did a great job of making it fun.

We paid our salespeople pretty well—$30,000 to $50,000 a year, in the eighties and nineties, which in most of the country was enough to buy a house and send your kids to college. We paid a little more in New York, L.A., San Francisco, and the like. Real hustlers earned up to $80,000. Our turnover rates were the lowest in the business. We were extremely proud of our benefits package, especially health care, where, as self-insureds, we made sure we covered our people better than anybody in the retail industry. We also installed a tiered system where employees who needed the most help, like single mothers with children, paid the lowest percentage share of costs on their premiums.

You know the old canard about how the customer is always first? That's not the way we played it at the Men's Wearhouse. In our view, the employee was number one. It's just always been a first principle with me, a golden rule thing for me as an employer. I'd like to think that taking care of our employees was an extension of my personality, of my countercultural life ethic, of wanting to bring that sixties sensibility of love into everything I did, especially my business.

Over the years, I took the time to honor thousands of our employees with personalized notes, generated by customer calls to my office that praised their work. I'd have a couple of secretaries in our Houston headquarters listen to the calls and write up specific response letters to the employee on my stationery—"From the Desk of George Zimmer." Like, everybody talks about customer service. We actually used it to send positive feedback to the employee. When I traveled around the country to visit our stores, I saw many of these notes framed and hanging on the walls. It was just a little thing that I felt very good about, something that set us apart from most of corporate America.

Now that I'm years removed from managing the company, I wonder sometimes if maybe I could have been more union friendly. You look at today's problem of wealth inequality, and there is no question that the weaker unions became, the more the disparity between the rich and poor grew.

I can only think of one unionization effort we ever faced—which was defeated—when they tried to organize our main warehouse in Houston. I told unions to have at it. Then our workers voted fair and square not to unionize. Another time we got caught up as a third party when the Teamsters, I think it was, made a move on one of our suppliers up in Canada. I had no problem with it. In fact, I told the company to clean up its act when I found out that some of their employees had lodged some serious and credible complaints.

For years, I did a little dance with Bruce Raynor, the former boss of the garment and hotel workers' unions. Raynor, of course, became famous when his union's successful organization efforts in North Carolina inspired *Norma Rae*, which won the Academy Award for Best Picture. Raynor thought he could turn me like he did a few other CEOs to open up to the union. I just didn't trust him, and we never signed an agreement. Which is probably why he threw up a couple of informational pickets at me, including one when I attended a fundraiser at the Oakland Zoo and his people held up signs that read, "George Zimmer Cares More about Animals Than People." Ouch.

From the time we hired our first three employees, we wanted to make sure they were getting a better deal than what they'd been getting before.

Before I'd ever heard of terms like "stakeholder capitalism" or "conscious capitalism," I knew that to gain the trust of our employees, to capture their loyalty, we'd be nuts to try and squeeze every last nickel out of them. It's just bad for business. We've always thought that taking care of our people is good for business. It's also just plain old good. We've never wanted our employees to fear us. We loved them. Maybe it was just another example of that reverse Machiavellian impulse—love over fear, instead of fear over love—that overcame me before I'd ever even read *The Prince*.

• • •

We believed that the employee was the ambassador to the customer, and if you wanted the customer to be happy, you had to make sure the employee was happy first.

Back in the beginning, I'd tell the wardrobe consultants, "Look, I'm not going to tell you that you have to smile when you greet the customer. I just want you to know that the authenticity of your experience is the thing that's going to influence the transaction and the degree to which that customer is going to want to return to our store. If you're smiling because somebody told you to, the customer will pick up on that, and they will spot you for a phony." You can't force happiness. I'd tell the floor people to remember the one thing that all our customers had in common: they were mammals. And one thing that mammals are pretty good at is picking up on phony messaging, no matter the species.

Every year, our executive team would create sales goals for each of our individual stores (which became quite an undertaking once we had several hundred of them). But these weren't just static numbers. The district managers would take them back to the regional managers, who would give them to the store managers, who would have meetings with their sales staff every February. We'd let the frontline salespeople work the number for at least a few days to determine whether it was realistic. If they didn't feel they could hit it, we could adjust. We didn't just dangle these things like carrots in front of a rabbit, making the rabbit chase something it could never catch. We *wanted* the salespeople to hit their number and get their bonus. We wanted them to ring the bell. We knew that in order to achieve the best year-end outcome, they had to be fully invested in the goal. For the employees to buy into the goal, they had to believe they could reach it.

Overwhelmingly, they did. During my time at the Men's Wearhouse, some 85 percent of our employees received a bonus every year, and fully a fifth of those got the super bonus for beating their number to a pulp.

I made a mistake in the early days of the Men's Wearhouse, when we didn't pay commissions. Back then, I believed that people always wanted to do their best for its own simple sake. I hate to say it, but that was the counterculture talking, my inner hippie, stirred in a sixties roux that thought the whole concept of commissions was dehumanizing. Well, it took me about ten years to get over myself on that.

"You know, George," more than one member of my staff used to tell me, "that's not human nature. Money motivates people." Giving in to the idea of commissions was the beginning of my transformation into a true CEO. Yes, most people were good, decent human beings, but they were better salespeople if they worked on a commission. Ours started at 3 percent and grew to 7 percent at $500.

But taking care of our employees meant a whole lot more than money. It was about respecting them and trusting them. We didn't run criminal background checks on them when they came in the front door. In fact, some of our best salespeople came in with "jackets," as we came to learn. They did know how to hustle, after all. We didn't make anybody take drug tests, unless the law required it for drivers and the like. We allowed our employees to donate their unused sick time to each other. We gave our people fully paid three-week sabbaticals every five years, on top of their regular vacation benefits, to go visit their ancestral homelands or just take a deep breath. Or they could take it in one-week increments, if they liked. We also distributed about $10 million in college scholarships over the decades to the children of our employees through the Zimmer Family Foundation.

We trained the hell out of everybody in our company. At the grassroots level, we created what we called Suits University, and we ran thousands and thousands of our employees through it, thirty-five at a time, at our Bay Area office, from all over the country. The main thing we taught at these weeklong sessions was our concept of "selling with soul." It was a pretty simple idea: don't look at the customer as a way to make money. See him as a human being who has clothing needs that you are going to help him figure out.

Our managers, we rounded them up in groups of fifty for training sessions in Atlanta, Detroit, and, most famously for us, Pajaro Dunes along Monterey Bay on the central coast of California, where our vice president of corporate culture, Julie Panaccione, had a line on a beach house. Basically, it was just a party, with plenty of booze, football on the beach, nights around the fire pit, shooting pool, talking shop. When we got too big, we moved to the Chaminade resort in Santa Cruz where the training sessions that lasted until 6 PM gave way to the real learning and bonding that occurred. First in the restaurant, then in the bar.

We trained our managers to listen to the rank-and-file. We had company barbecues where we did the Cupid Shuffle, we put together company sports teams, and we bought season tickets to sports in every city and made sure our managers distributed them to our line employees. And we had the massive holiday parties, about a dozen of which I attended every year. I made a point every year of visiting as many as a third of our stores, and of having my picture taken with as many employees as possible. My being something of a TV celebrity, for whatever that was worth, seemed to mean something to them. I think it gave them a sense of pride and loyalty to tell their friends and family that they worked for that guy in the commercials who said "I guarantee it."

I totally bought into the concept of "servant leadership" as laid down by Robert Greenleaf of AT&T back before I'd ever dreamed of starting the Men's Wearhouse. I was there to serve the company, to serve the employees, and I made sure at the company parties, and on my visits to the stores, that I was one of them.

I liked that almost all of the thousands of employees I encountered felt comfortable enough to know me as just a regular guy, not some far-off diviner of the company fate. I liked it, too, that most of them knew me as "George."

Anybody who's ever owned a store knows about the fairly serious problem of employee theft. I think the average loss to the retail industry was something like 2 percent a year. Most of the time I was in charge of the Men's Wearhouse, our inventory shrinkage ran at a rate of about 0.5 percent. For the $2 billion company that we were, the 1.5 percent difference meant $30 million. Rather than stuff the savings in our pockets, we spent it in celebration of the honesty and loyalty of our workforce.

• • •

Rolling into the late eighties, we blistered the competition with our cost-comparative commercials. The big boys got so mad they sued.

I started it off with a stand-up in front of a blue map of the United States, dapper as usual in a brand-name suit (but without the label). By this time, people knew me as the "I guarantee it" guy. Now I was stacking us up against the most prominent stores in their hometowns, in one-on-one matchups where we called out the competition by name.

"The more we shop the competition, the better we look," I said, happily. The spot flipped to a still shot of a model in a suit. "Our price. Theirs," I intoned, as we flashed the Men's Wearhouse $295 sticker price against the $380 they charged at Dayton's in Minneapolis. "Our price. Theirs." Boom, another wipeout, with a smiling gent flashing an arrangement that would have cost you $230 at Men's compared to the $345 at Rich's in Atlanta. "Our price. Theirs." Another winner, on a suit that we sold for $275 against the $450 they charged at Hudson's in Detroit. And on and on, all over the country. "The same manufacturers' suits are less at the Men's Wearhouse," I said in my closing argument, before signing off with, "I guarantee it."

Nobody could dispute it, although a couple of the biggest names in American retail took a crack at us on the technicalities in lawsuits filed in Northern California.

"Men's Wearhouse exposes the competition: Macy's," our narrator said in the ad that targeted the Goliath of our industry. The commercial picked up with me showing off a pair a mannequin torsos side-by-side, both of them looking sharp in the same suit. "This is the same wool blend that Macy's sells," I said. "It's the same material, the same designer, the same manufacturer. Everything's the same except the price: $265 at Macy's, $189 at the Men's Wearhouse—a $76 difference. Money that belongs in your pocket, not theirs."

Macy's and Nordstrom brought the legal actions against us. They argued that the suits weren't exactly the same, in that we didn't have the same label—even if everything else was a mirror image. We settled both cases out of court—no harm, no foul—and slightly altered our pitch while sticking to our basic appeal: you can still get the same suit at the Men's Wearhouse for a hell of a lot less.

I can only recall one other legal dust-up of any significance with our advertising. Like 18.5 million YouTube viewers, our creative people took a liking to the lovely Jack Johnson hit, "Better Together." They came up with a jingle that flowed beautifully into one of our pieces. The melody didn't exactly copy the Hawaiian singer-songwriter's brilliance note for note, but it shared enough similarity for Johnson's lawyers to give us a call. I thought there was enough distinction between the songs to keep us out of legal hot water, but why fight it? I told his lawyers, sure, we'll take the ad down and change the music, which we did. And just to make sure there were no hard feelings, I wrote a check for $50,000 to a charity of Jack Johnson's choice—better than spending all that money on lawyers. He agreed to my compromise idea, and it just goes to show there are plenty of inventive, win-win ways for reasonable people to stay out of the courtroom.

As our company grew, so did the effectiveness and sophistication of our TV commercials. The years added a touch of gray to my hair and beard, and I backed off on the hard-charging dude of my youth who jabbed you in the chest with his index finger to let you know that he meant it when he guaranteed it.

We added some very cool jazz riffs for our musical backdrop, sometimes just a cat on his stand-up bass going off into a controlled groove, with the drummer brushing the cymbals in an odd time. I relaxed through the shot with my arm stretched across the back of a couch, wearing a turtleneck under a sport coats instead of a tie. "Business casual" had become the new look. We added a new phrase that stretched my signature sign-off to "You're going to like the way you look. I guarantee it."

We reached out to women coming into the store to do the shopping for their men, on the premise that we could help them answer the question, "What do men want?" In these commercials, a gorgeous woman perused one of our stores, looking at shoes and ties—"essentials," I called them—as well as what I described as "more contemporary looks" while she felt up a black leather jacket.

"Because what men want, that's complicated," I said, while the picture moved on to the woman's boyfriend—wiggling around at play, in a sandbox, in a playground mini-tractor, like a goof.

I think it was also in the late eighties when we came up with might have been our most successful advertising piece.

We played off the famous *Star Wars* scroll, and we ran it the day after Christmas and every day for the entire month of January, when the HUT levels (TV advertising jargon for "homes using television") were at their highest, and we repeated it every year for about a decade. With my gravelly baritone reading the script that slipped off into infinity, we told America, "Once a year, and only once a year, the Men's Wearhouse has a sale, and this is it."

I've got to say, it did sound like I had the voice of God when I suggested to the public, "Save on hundreds of suits, sport coats, shirts, slacks, ties, and belts."

In the early nineties, as my gray hair overwhelmed the brown, we didn't cover up my age or embarrass ourselves by trying to make me look ridiculously hip. We embraced the sense of history that my advancing years projected. We let the hipster proclivities of our younger customers speak for themselves in our later advertising—the young white guy with a three-day-old beard, a mop of mussed hair over his forehead, the tattoo on his neck; a Black dude with short dreads, on the move, the jacket open on his black suit; dashing and dangerous thirty-somethings of every stripe getting out of cars, staring you down through windows, walking confidently down urban avenues doing business on cell phones in their slim-fits with narrow lapels on jackets that barely dropped below the belt. Nobody wore a tie, at least not one knotted to the top.

Over these figures, I went on in the voiceover about the cut of the man rather than the cut of the suit, "because today, it's not so much the brand of suit that defines the man as it is the brand of man who wears it."

Besides having gone full gray, I'd donned a pair of sunglasses. We shot this one with me behind the wheel of a car in Houston and Seattle, with a camera screwed into the hood, a cameraman sitting shotgun, another cameraman sitting in the back on the passenger side, and the director seated right behind me. He made it easy. He'd say the line and I would just repeat it. I didn't have to think about anything. We had the sound guy in the trunk, while the police in both cities held up traffic for us. Just like they did in the old, old days, when Harold Gunn dressed up like Charlie Chaplin and ran down the freeway chasing a runaway clothes rack.

•　•　•

I guess you could say that over the twenty-nine-year life of the commercials, I became something of a celebrity. TV talk shows invited me in as their guest. Every major newspaper in the country wrote stories about me and the rise of the Men's Wearhouse. I met a couple of presidents, while they were presidents. Business schools had me come speak to their classes. I shook hands with Stephen Stills and Manute Bol. The Dalai Lama even granted me a semi-private audience. (Later the same day, a

Tibetan scholar who introduced the Dalai Lama to a large gathering at Stanford University became overwhelmed in tearful emotion. In comforting the sobbing man, the Dalai Lama draped his arm around the man's shoulder and said, in broken English, "I knew your father. He would never be more proud of you." The expression of compassion was unforgettable, something I've never otherwise witnessed in my life. It brought me and everyone else in the room that day into a state of grace.) Everywhere I went, people recognized me, and they hit me every day with "I guarantee it." Never bothered me once. I'd like to think that most of the people who saw our ads felt the same way the Men's Wearhouse employees felt about the company, that they knew me.

By 1992, we felt it was time to test the proposition that we had become a comfortable presence in their lives. It was time to go public.

—| 6 |—

Going Public

Once a New Yorker, always a New Yorker, and I was a New Yorker, even though I'd been on the move my whole adult life, from St. Louis to Dallas to Houston and, by April 1992, to Oakland. New York is in my DNA, same as it is for anybody who was born there or lived an appreciable segment of their lives in the city that never sleeps. Even from Scarsdale, some twenty miles to the north, where I spent the majority of my upbringing, I always felt pulled back to the city, to my grandparents' homes on the Upper West and Upper East sides. I still feel the tug.

As a kid, I must have gone to five hundred baseball and football games at Yankee Stadium. I did some time at Shea Stadium, too, and the Polo Grounds, and Ebbets Field, where I enjoyed watching the Boys of Summer (maybe even more than the Yankees). Name a Broadway musical, and I'll bet I can sing the showstopper. If I didn't see everything that ever played in the late fifties and early sixties—*Oklahoma*, *West Side Story*, *Bye Bye Birdie*, *Carousel*, and *Barefoot in the Park* starring Robert Redford—well, I came pretty damn close, thanks to my grandmother scoring us seats from her work as a costume designer.

I sat through a couple of Macy's Thanksgiving Day parades. I trembled in awe inside the massive concourse of Grand Central Station, which seemed to the youthful me the biggest indoor space in the universe. Mayor Robert F. Wagner, Jr., intrigued me. So did John Lindsay. I went to the 1964 World's Fair. Nobody asked me, but in my opinion, you'll never find a better rare roast beef sandwich than the ones you used to get at the Carnegie and Stage delicatessens. I still order bagels from Zabars. I spent days of my life in the American Museum of Natural History.

I've always identified with New York's history, its traditions, its icons, and they are as much a part of me as anything I've done, or anywhere I've been, from the college hippie who questioned authority in St. Louis to the entrepreneur who started up a little men's clothing store in Houston.

You can imagine, then, the electrical charge that shot like lightning out of my toes and fingertips the day that I stood in the interior balcony at the New York Stock Exchange, when I looked across the trading floor at hundreds of blue jackets as they brokered their final transactions of the day, one of the strangest and most thrilling days of my life.

At my command, they would soon come to a halt. I was about to do something that was far beyond my childhood dreams. I'd been to this vortex of capitalism on occasion with my grandfather, Papa George, but I'd never done anything like I was about to do at 4 PM, on the afternoon of Oct. 2, 2000, when, to my lasting amazement, I rang the closing bell.

Sure, it might have been an odd place for a son of the sixties to find some affirmation. But since going into business for myself, I'd been trying to use the platform of enterprise to promote what I perceived as the values of that era—treating humans with dignity, rethinking the way so much money goes to the top, benefiting the wider community and the environment. Could I do it from inside the breastplate of the world's greatest testament to shareholder capitalism? The answer, I hoped, was yes, although it would require a shift in the paradigm: *from* serving more than just the interests of investment banks and insurance companies that dominate the shareholder class, *to* promoting the general welfare of workers, the environment, and the wider community, without which the forces of capital cannot survive.

Papa George would have never believed it, me standing on the NYSE balcony. Over the decades, this same spot has been occupied by dignitaries ranging from Nelson Mandela to Ronald Reagan, Sarah Jessica Parker to "Sully" Sullenberger, Joe DiMaggio to Darth Vader. I'd never ended apartheid or landed a damaged plane in the Hudson River, but there I was. The Men's Wearhouse had officially arrived. In this case, all we'd done was switch over from our previous sinecure at the less-traditional Nasdaq to begin trading our stock in the more staid hall of the New York Stock Exchange. What the hell, it was an unbelievable honor for a company headed by a native New Yorker. Even with some deep questions about the role of corporatism in American society, I happily accepted it.

Earlier in the day, I had emceed a fashion show on Wall Street, right outside the iconic exterior granite columns of the NYSE building. The runway belonged to the best offerings of the Men's Wearhouse, and I got a little help with the commentating from a cohost who also was familiar on the airwaves: Phil Rizzuto, the Hall of Fame shortstop from the New York Yankees, and one of the great sports heroes of my youth. As a kid, Rizzuto and the great Yankee dynasty of the Casey Stengel years brought me into baseball cognizance. I remember seeing Rizzuto start a few double plays and lay down some sacrifice bunts. Mostly, though, I knew him as the voice of the club when he became a Yankee announcer at the end of his playing days. For a Scarsdale kid who identified with the city, doing *anything* as a co-whatever with Phil Rizzuto rose to the level of an out-of-body experience.

Another emcee shared the stage with Rizzuto and me for that day's fashion show: NYSE chairman and chief executive Richard A. "Dick" Grasso. A few years later, the NYSE board forced him out over a controversially enormous $140 million compensation package. I can't say it was that much of a dream to be standing next to Grasso. But it was surreal.

We ate lunch in the red-carpeted NYSE boardroom that runs the length of the building, and I was taken by the famous seven-foot-tall Fabergé urn, a token of Czar Nicholas II's appreciation for the billion-dollar package the NYSE board put together for him in 1904 to build Russia a nationwide railway system. The train didn't do him much good when the Bolsheviks rode him out on a rail in 1918. Despite the czar's 1918 execution, the board kept the egg.

I'll let you in on a little secret: nobody actually *rings* the bell. All you do is push a button, which was totally okay with me. I would have been okay with anything. Opening bell, closing bell, halftime bell—ringing it, banging it, clanging it, whatever it took. This was the New York Stock Exchange, dammit, and, to add to the glory of the moment, I was standing on the balcony next to the man who had done more for me than anybody else in my life—my father, Robert E. Zimmer, who was now the senior vice president in charge of real estate of the Men's Wearhouse. Shot down by the Nazis, survivor of the stalag, his presence with me, the prodigal hippie son, above the Pit was absolutely humbling and exhilarating. My brother was also up there with us. Jim by then had become senior vice president of merchandising for the Men's Wearhouse. This was our blood.

And this was our time—as far as the arrival of the Men's Wearhouse as a true force in the American economy was concerned, the eagle had landed. That was us up there, the Zimmer men, and this was our company.

We did have a lot of help. Some of the most important members of our team were right there with us. They included my frat brother Harry Levy, my twenty-seven-year partner Richie Goldman, and our old consultant, who had since become our chief financial officer and maybe my best friend in the world, Dave Edwab. We rang the bell, and it clanged the day's work to a close, and we all clapped the way all the executive teams do when they get up there on the balcony. We soaked it in.

The company that I had envisioned while driving home in a fury in the middle of the night, after the Foley's episode in Houston some twenty-seven years in the past, had taken its place on the most prominent trading floor in the world, in New York, New York.

• • •

Our road to the big time began eight years before we sounded the NYSE bell, when we announced our initial public offering on the Nasdaq exchange. No bell-ringing there. No celebration to speak of. No trading floor, even. The only thing we got out of them was an expectation that we'd grow like hell. We were happy to accommodate.

Nasdaq welcomed companies like ours, a start-up, which fit in fine in the volatile world of entrepreneurial experimentation. We weren't Macy's or the Federated. Nasdaq investors like to see major growth; we needed to do that, and then we needed to plow everything we made into creating even more growth. Unlike the NYSE, shareholders on the Nasdaq knew not to expect dividends.

On the eve of taking our act to the Nasdaq, nineteen years in, the Men's Wearhouse was still mostly me, a collection of smart friends, a father who'd come to believe in me, a talented brother, and a late mother who'd acted contrary to her better judgment when she took a $500,000 chance on me.

We had done pretty damn well for ourselves by the time we hung our-selves out there in 1992 in the public-investment marketplace. Convinced our business model was a winner, we jumped on the accelerator. We did it with the assistance of Bear Stearns when the Wall Street investment banking titan was at its apex, eighteen years before the winds of financial destruction told the world in 2008 that no son of a bitch is too big to fail. Bear went down first, and hard, followed by Stearns' twin in the Wall Street monument to shareholder capitalism, Lehman Brothers, and the two of them damn near took the entire American economy down with them.

At the time we went public, we felt it was the only way to obtain the huge kind of cash infusion we needed to grow. I knew it would also present a major challenge for us to stay true to who we were and what we had been doing from when we first set up our little adult lemonade stand on Westheimer Road in Houston, when I talked about "nurturing creativity" and "striving toward becoming self-actualized people" a la Abraham Maslow, on the back of a cocktail napkin. Now, here we were, ready to submit these humble objectives to the demands of Wall Street. Would our investors—our shareholders—allow us to achieve the pinnacle of Maslow's hierarchy of needs?

Back when we made our first overtures to Bear Stearns, our empire had grown to 113 stores, still confined mostly to Texas, California, and the Pacific Northwest, with a few outposts scattered elsewhere in the United States. Infused with cash put up by the mutual funds and other investors, our sales by the end of 1992 had reached $170 million a year, and our net earnings had climbed to $5.9 million. Small potatoes, for sure, but the trend line promised greater success.

We added thirty-one new stores in our first year as a public company, probably twice as many as we'd opened during any single year of our previous history.

Me, I was mainly just the face and front man and the chief strategic thinker of the now-public operation. All I did was sell suits and make TV commercials and envision the future. The guy who ran the numbers, the one who probably helped more than anybody to push us, who fully participated in the transformation of the Men's Wearhouse into a national retail powerhouse, the one who deserves a substantial amount of the credit for what we became—I think you've got to give a whole hell of a lot of it to David Edwab, our contract consultant, who helped us find our way out of the mess when one of those Texas banks called our loan.

I'd been talking to Dave for years about taking the Men's Wearhouse public. He told me over and over again that when the timing was right, he'd come aboard as our chief financial officer. The way I saw it, I'd make the commercials, he'd do the numbers, and we'd conquer the men's clothing retail world. In late 1991, it felt like the moment had arrived, and I hired David as the Men's Wearhouse CFO. I would later promote him to chief operating officer, and then to president; I would eventually put him on our board of directors, and he and I would become best friends. We would take vacations together with our wives and families to Hawaii and Lake Tahoe.

Maybe more than anybody else, Dave shared my understanding of the company's potential. If anything, he was even more enthusiastic about our future. He saw that we were crushing it with our promise of quality, service, and a good price, our understanding of men's thinking—or, more accurately, their non-thinking—when it came to shopping for their own clothes. Of course, we also had integrity and appeal baked into our advertising. He knew we were sitting on a gold mine. We agreed that taking this thing national couldn't miss, that our model would work from Aliquippa to Alabama, anywhere there were ... men. The only thing we needed to do was raise money. Then it would be over the Sierra to the Rockies, and across the plains to the Appalachians, from coast to coast to coast.

It was Dave who got us into Bear Stearns, through his friendship with the head of the firm's Dallas office, Sheldon Stein, a Brooklyn native and Harvard-trained lawyer. I remember before they signed on as our underwriter, Bear Stearns had a guy interview me for a half hour about my sense of right and wrong. At the time, the interview seemed fairly innocuous and polite—pro forma, really. Decades later, it struck me as kind of ironic that a company that proved to be unscrupulous to the point of nearly destroying the American economy would have the audacity to ask anybody about their business ethics, about their moral character. These are the guys who packaged trash mortgages into indistinguishable heaps of investment rubbish, stoking the worst economic crisis between the Great Depression and the coronavirus.

But in 1992, I was more than happy to answer any and all questions that they asked as long as it would set us up for our IPO. Dave was my guy, and Dave was tight with Shelley, and I felt they had my back. So, the three of us went out on our pre-IPO tour, in private jets that Bear Stearns lined up (and that we paid for, including the flight attendants who were brought along to serve just the three of us). We stayed in the best hotels (our tab again) and ate in the finest restaurants in the country (on us, of course), as we made our pitch to some 150 investors about the coming greatness of the Men's Wearhouse. New York, Boston, Philly, Detroit, Minneapolis, Chicago, Dallas, San Francisco, Denver—two cities a day, first class all the way. All the splurging felt a bit wasteful, but this was a public offering, and this is how they work: image is important. I felt, then, that it was just something we had to do to let them know that we were for real.

Our day at Nasdaq came in April 1992—without pomp, or circumstance, only an announcement and an offer.

They valued us to the tune of $12.7 million, modest compared to some of the eye poppers you see nowadays. Taking inflation into account, our IPO score only amounts to 12 percent of the average $184 million that Nasdaq's new entries generated in 2019. Altogether, we sold 2,531,250 shares that went for a little more than five bucks each. We had offered 3,375,000 shares at $5.78.

Even if the result was underwhelming, it was enough to get us rolling, to begin the financing of a steady expansion that would take us into the next millennium.

• • •

On the precipice of monumental growth, I knew that I needed to look outside myself and my tight circle of confidantes to find guidance for the Men's Wearhouse and its future. In our rag-tag expansion thus far, I'd been doing a lot of flying by the seat of my pants, going on instinct. But heading a public company was uncharted territory. I wanted deep thinkers who shared my sixties sensibilities. People who believed as I did that our ascendancy would rise from a foundation of strong business ethics and a sense that we could do things better for the world as well as ourselves.

Despite my success as an entrepreneur, as a commercial pitch man, and as a growing giant of men's retail, I never strayed from the idealism of my days in the counterculture. Even in 1992, if you had asked me, "But weren't you a dope-smoking hippie, George?" I would answer that question with an unqualified yes. Hell, yes, I had been a hippie, and as far as I was concerned, I still was. I certainly still smoked dope, anyway. Maybe I did wear a suit and a tie, the uniform of the establishment, to work every day. Maybe I now sold that uniform to the masses. But the same thing we said back in the sixties whenever anybody over thirty ragged on us about our long hair: it's not what's on your head, we'd say, it's what's in it, and also what's going on in your heart and soul. Even if your hair was shorter than it used to be, and even if you traded in your tie-dyed T-shirt for a tie. And I knew then, like I know now, that nothing matters more than the Golden Rule—you do unto others same as you'd want them to do unto you. Sure, I competed hard from the very beginning, even started the Men's Wearhouse motivated more than a little by vengeance, behaviors not typically associated with the Summer of Love. But I never lost sight of

our core mission, where we promoted love over fear and succeeded enough
to make the corporate world notice.

Around the same time that the Men's Wearhouse went public, the
country was benefiting from a little burst of progressivism, when Bill
Clinton put an end to twelve years of Republican rule. In the years before,
I had begun to read about people and businesses and nongovernmental
organizations that looked for ways to meld the interests of the entrepreneur with those of the surrounding society. Wanting to learn more,
I sought out like-minded thinkers on matters of commerce and social
consciousness. They included luminaries such as Willis Harman, a futurist
writer and researcher who was big on the Human Potential Movement,
which sought to give everybody in the species a shot at being the best
version of themselves. There was Rinaldo Brutoco, the Canadian-born
businessman, writer, and founder of the California Public Interest Law
Center. Finally, Michael Ray, a professor at the Stanford Graduate School
of Business who was teaching an explosively popular class in Silicon Valley
called "Personal Creativity in Business."

The four of us believed that the creation of progressive, enlightened,
spiritual, and humanistic business enterprises represented the last, best hope
of the world. Looking around at governments of all sorts, all around the
world, we concluded that they were overburdened and inadequate, corrupted
by greed and self-interest and broken politics. Schools didn't teach, health
care didn't heal, and the homeless roamed the earth. Worldwide income
inequality had stripped half the world, it seemed, of its basic needs. Amid so
much failure, we saw the business sector as the only viable institution left in
society. Of course, you could make the argument that many of the inequities
of the world resulted from the exploitations of business. We recognized that.
We just didn't believe that it had to be that way, and we believed that the
only way it could turn around for workers, for the environment, for society
as a whole would be for the business community to establish and live up to
a standard of responsibility and impeccability.

With this responsibility in mind, we formed an organization we called
the World Business Academy—Brutoco and Harman as cofounders, myself
as a founding trustee, and Ray as a research fellow. Our founding mission
was nothing short of inspiring businesses to look beyond their sole pursuit
of profits to assume responsibility for the whole of society, and to help those
who shared our values to create a better world by putting on conferences

to showcase research into topics we cared about: visionary leadership and sustainable energy development, organizational behavior and culture transformation, marketing and new product diffusion, organic food systems, and mindful business practices, to name a few.

The group's research so impressed me that when the Men's Wearhouse went public, I asked Rinaldo Brutoco if he'd like to join our board. He accepted. So did Michael Ray, who had already attracted notice as one of the leading influencers of business talent in the emerging technological Shangri-La of Silicon Valley. The two of them also seemed to harbor deeply spiritual sides, something that I had been developing myself over the course of my life.

I liked the metaphysical edge that Rinaldo and Michael added to our board. I've always believed that you learn as a business from people who come from different places, and these two men, along with the thinking of Willis Harman, gave us a whole new range of experiences and perspectives that I thought were crucial in establishing the Men's Wearhouse as more than just another company that only sought to enrich its shareholders. With their input, I thought we could present the Men's Wearhouse as a company that lived the types of sustainable values we were all talking about. I wanted the Men's Wearhouse to become more than just a business that sold clothes to men. I thought that we could turn it into an experiment, a laboratory to test a range of hypotheses on how to enrich the lives of our workers, take care of our suppliers, and improve the communities in which we operated. I knew that we could do this, and at the same time make a few bucks for ourselves and our shareholders.

• • •

The cash infusion from going public supercharged our growth. Within two years, we increased our advertising budget to $23 million a year, on its way to more than $30 million by later in the nineties. Soon as we finished the IPO, we added one store a week for the rest of the century, all over the country. Since the first offering worked out to our benefit, it only made sense that we go back to the well. Over the next three years we conducted additional offerings that raised $59.6 million, about half for the selling shareholders and half for the company.

My father, as much as I loved him, gave me a little bit of a heart attack before one of the secondary offerings when he told the people at Bear

Stearns that he wasn't interested in selling at the agreed-upon market price of $15.25 a share. I tried to talk some sense into him. I told him it was pretty damn unfair to hold out for more once we'd agreed on a price for a public offering. He didn't listen to me, nor did he listen to any of the underwriters at Bear Stearns. He insisted that he could do better if he held out now and sold later on his own.

I would see a lot of this kind of recalcitrance over the years as I bought up stores to fold into the Men's Wearhouse empire, usually from guys about my father's age. I called it "old man syndrome"—an affliction that hits men in their seventies, who became sentimental about some little piece of something that they built or had held from its inception. They'd ask me, "You think I'm just going to give this store away?"

Bear Stearns, in its effort to work my dad, called in its own old man from out of the bullpen. In came the legendary Alan C. "Ace" Greenberg, to close out my pop. Greenberg had risen like an Oklahoma whirlwind from the state he grew up in to take charge of the Wall Street giant back in the seventies. He came into the firm in 1949 as a clerk who monitored oil drilling activity, before he took his gambler's instinct to the trading floor in his off hours and caught the eye of one of the partners who promoted him to arbitrageur. Greenberg soon became the head of the arbitrage department, on his way to a partnership, and then, for fifteen years, to CEO of the company. Later he was named its executive chairman.

None of it impressed Robert E. Zimmer. Ace Greenberg failed to convince. My father still refused to sell, until a year later, when he attracted a dollar more per share selling his Men's Wearhouse stock on the open market. Honestly, too bad for him he didn't hold out a little longer. Our stock price caught fire, and by February 1997, it had risen to $38.50 a share.

On one of those secondary offerings, which involved more jet-setting across the country, on a trip to Dallas, I had to pay a visit to history, which has always been a passion of mine, especially the history that I felt I had lived, such as the assassination of President John F. Kennedy.

A limo picked us up at the airport and pulled into the Adolphus Hotel, downtown. As the rest of the posse piled out, I asked the driver, "Could you give me a quick run over to Dealey Plaza?" It was five minutes away. I needed to take in the scene of the crime of the previous century, the spot where on November 22, 1963, the thirty-fifth president of the United States was shot and killed. I figured as long as I was in the neighborhood, I should give the area a look-see, to try and understand why questions still lingered after more than three decades as to whether Lee Harvey Oswald acted alone in the assassination. The limo driver took me down Main Street to Houston Street, left, past the schoolbook depository building, onto Elm Street—the assassination street—through the chute leading below the railroad underpass. For the first time in my life, I felt the immediacy of the shooting. I gained a deeper understanding of the absolutely close proximity of the president's motorcade to the grassy knoll to his right where conspiracy buffs contend that a second gunman took him out from behind a stone fence.

I had the driver spin me through there a second time, and I left Dallas knowing in my own mind that we still haven't received the whole truth about the death of the president.

• • •

By the mid-nineties, the Men's Wearhouse had shifted into overdrive. The adult lemonade stand had transformed itself into a major modern retailer—international, even, in outlook. We saw the future and responded in real time, big time. We'd seen the mountaintop, and it belonged to us: we were the king of what we called in our Security and Exchange Commission filings the "off-price" specialists in "men's tailored business attire," selling suits, slacks, sport coats, shirts, shoes, and everything else anywhere from 30 to 50 percent less than big department stores and high-end men's shops. Tapping further into this market, in 1996 we opened a wholly owned subsidiary we called Value Priced Clothing. It could sell you a suit for as little as $99, in twenty-five stores in four states.

The industry had consolidated. As it got smaller, we got bigger. As we got bigger, we increased our buying power. As we increased our buying power, we created a more predictable relationship with our vendors. As things became more predictable, all the popular designers wanted in with us—Pierre Cardin, Botany 500, Yves Saint Laurent, Cricketeer, and Joseph & Feiss International. As the big-name brands came in through our doors, we sent their garments out on the backs of our regular customers at our everyday low prices. As we sold more suits, we leveraged our market share to sign direct-sourcing agreements with 20 percent of our 180 vendors. As we signed more deals with overseas manufacturers, we struggled to keep as much of our production as possible within the borders of the United States, with not much success.

Same time as we got fancy with the designer labels, we saw that overall and everywhere, men's clothing tastes had changed. You almost never saw anybody wear a suit to a baseball game anymore. We adapted to the trend toward "business casual." A lot of our competitors panicked at the switch. We rolled with the flow. We stocked up on mock turtlenecks, sport coats, and sweaters, and we sold them like crazy.

Big-name stores that ignored the trend away from formality did so at their own risk, as we saw in the nineties when one regional men's clothing icon after another collapsed. This occurred in the face of our progress.

A few of them we snatched up, before they closed their doors, or after they'd filed for bankruptcy. There's no question, we had competed very hard with these companies. If there's a way of reconciling putting them out of business with the ideals of stakeholder capitalism, we can say that we hired many of our former competitors' employees, and that we paid them more. We can also say that we gave their old customers better deals. We gave their suppliers a fair look, and I think the overall community benefited.

These other stores were weakened, and they knew it. Some of them, it took a little longer for them to come around to the realization that their day was done. Eventually, more than a hundred different ownership concerns succumbed in the face of our growth, from decently sized regional chains to stores that had been the only game in their town. Until we came along. I think the only store that survived us was some guy in Salt Lake City, a Mormon, backed by other Mormons who didn't mind paying an extra hundred dollars or more for a suit. (One of the casualties was Foley's, the department chain in Houston that did me wrong back in 1973. They went out of business in 2006.)

We went head-to-head in the Southern California market against what had been the league leader down there in our field. By the end of 1996, we'd battered C&R Clothiers, an even-lower cost competitor, into bankruptcy. We acquired seventeen of their stores, as well as their distribution center.

We acquired and liquidated Kuppenheimer, a retail brand in Chicago and Atlanta that had fallen on hard times, largely as a result of our success.

We took over the four Walter Pye's stores in Houston and one each in San Antonio and New Orleans.

We bought out the Suit Warehouse and their four stores in Detroit, but not until we had to go through a nasty legal fracas; they sued us over our name, which led to a spat in the judge's chambers in which our own Dave Edwab—a big guy, at six foot three and 275 pounds—ripped the arm off a chair and challenged their lawyer to take their disagreement into the street. Dave cooled off, and we reached a settlement to resolve the Suit Warehouse vs. Men's Wearhouse standoff.

We picked up thirty-three stores on a buyout of the Atlanta-based K&G chain.

In our biggest catch of the decade, we went into Canada and took over Moores Clothing for Men and folded their 107 stores into the Men's Wearhouse empire.

In our acquisitions strategy, we kind of flipped the script. Usually, you'd want to buy stores where the market was strong, the economy healthy. I held a diametrically opposed view. I liked to pick up bargains in places that might be on hard times but looked due for a turnaround. As a result, we signed better deals, hired more experienced people, took advantage of labor markets where we could pick and choose. Plus, we negotiated great rates on our television commercials, sometimes getting way more bang for our buck in markets where we were already on the air.

We didn't just pick over the bones of our dying competitors. We also opened new stores on our own, everywhere. We looked for storefronts in more affordable strip malls that were close to but not in shopping malls—our customers didn't like them. Our customers knew what they wanted, didn't need to do any browsing at other stores. Our customers didn't like the hassle of crowds. Our customers liked the close access and easier parking of strip malls—they could get in and out in the same time it might take you to buy a hamburger at In-N-Out. Not that we were fast food. We gave you the fashion equivalent of a nice steak, only it cost you 20 percent less to eat.

I put my father in charge of our real estate department, and there was nobody whom I trusted more in that job. He and I together signed off on the selection of three hundred new store sites.

Another thing about all these new stores: the volume in each of them was blasting off. We did about $880,000 per store a year before we went public. By the end of the nineties, the number had grown to $2 million.

As we grew, we integrated our management information and telecommunication systems. Under my frat brother Harry Levy's guidance, we

automatically replenished everything that everybody bought. We shifted
busywork onto computer systems and allowed our actual people to maximize
their analytical skills. We actually created a human resources department,
and we called it the Department of Corporate Culture. We added organizational infrastructure. We stepped up our training, our hiring, our promotions
of our best talent to supervisory positions, management positions, executive
positions.

As we skyrocketed into retail stardom in the nineties, for the first time
in the history of the Men's Wearhouse, I noticed that I was actually becoming wealthy. In fact, I had become a millionaire, even though I didn't draw a
salary—I just sold that stock that kept increasing in value. I bought a home
in the leafy enclave of Piedmont in the hills above Oakland. I could also
afford to realize a dream of buying and building on some beachfront property on the Big Island of Hawaii.

Not like I had that much time to enjoy my life as a beachcomber. I was
now into my third decade of six- and seven-day work weeks. But to be honest, I loved it. There was nothing I'd rather do.

I didn't have much of an inkling yet, but with our growth, with our
going public, I had put into place the mechanisms that would take me down
and force me out of the Men's Wearhouse and lead to its bankruptcy. And
some of these great minds, and one very close friend, would be the ones to
pull the levers.

7

Paradigm Shifts

L ike the rest of the country, the Men's Wearhouse struggled to get back on its feet in the months after the terrorist attacks of September 11, 2001. We wrestled with the loss of nearly three thousand of our fellow citizens, and on top of that the collapse of the American economy. The Men's Wearhouse felt the gut punch as much as anybody in the retail sector when our sales dropped by 20 percent in the fourth quarter.

With a fog of uncertainty still hovering over the country, I considered cancelling what had become a great tradition over the years at the Men's Wearhouse—our annual holiday parties. We'd been throwing them for years, these massive multimedia productions at scattered locations across the country, making them accessible to almost everybody who worked for the company. They were the fun part of our "work hard, play hard" credo, and we didn't do them on the cheap.

They were black tie all the way, and if you or your date couldn't afford a tux, we'd fit you up in one for free—easy enough for us, since we owned a million of them, which we rented primarily for weddings and proms. We hired limos to pick you up, and then we'd put you up in the four-star hotel where we pitched the ball. We served dinner, with the bar open before, during, and long after the meal, as we danced past the midnight hour. We'd throw about fifty of these things over the last six weeks of the year. I would personally attend at least a dozen of them every year.

I loved the holiday parties as much as anything I did across my forty years with the Men's Wearhouse. I loved to bond with our employees, to dine and dance with them, to get a feel for them, to get to know them by the thousands. Every year, they renewed the sense that I was doing something right in the world, providing good jobs that allowed good people to make good livings, by taking a nickel from the stockholders and distributing it downward in the form of a good time for our exceedingly valuable employees.

After dinner, I always delivered a speech—the holiday highlight for me. Dressed in my tux, I'd go out onto the dance floor with a microphone in one hand and maybe an iced coffee in the other, beneath the disco ball. I would first thank these incredible employees for the fantastic work they had done over the previous year. Then, I segued into the pep talk, to pump them up for the fabulous work we knew they'd be doing in the year ahead. It was all very motivational. What we needed, going into holiday season 2001, was something else—something inspirational.

With our sales in the dumps, and the country in a somber mood, and with me in need of some mood therapy, I got my own little jolt of inspiration from my old Washington University student body president. By this time, Ben Zaricor had become the chief executive of the fabulously successful Good Earth Tea Co. in Santa Cruz. Besides concocting some of the most interesting tea blends in the world, Ben had picked up a fairly interesting hobby over the years: collecting flags. He had about 3,500 of them, sourced from all over the world, and he'd even been profiled in publications as esteemed as the *Washington Post*.

A few weeks before the holiday parties, I told Ben I was thinking about cancelling them. As I bemoaned the state of the world, Ben stroked his chin and advised me to hold on before I did anything rash. "You've got to see this as an opportunity," he told me.

It just so happened that Ben had just the thing to turn my head around, to inspire the hard-working, loyal, dedicated employees of the Men's Wearhouse. It was a prop, he said, a real-life flag that had adorned the train station in Buffalo, New York, when the casket of Abraham Lincoln stopped for a few hours on its trip from Washington, DC, to the assassinated president's final resting place in Springfield, Illinois. He offered the banner for its inspirational symbolism, this flag that in 1865 waved over multitudes of grieving Americans in western New York who came out to cherish a final moment with their president, who had been murdered six days after the Union prevailed in the Civil War. Ben thought that 146 years later, the same flag might rally the spirit of a work force in those first few months after the deadly terrorist attacks in New York, Washington, and the airspace over rural Pennsylvania had plunged the nation into a new uncertainty.

I thought it was a great idea. It helped that I was a huge fan of Abraham Lincoln. The flag would serve as a memento from another time when our nation grieved yet persevered.

So, over the final six weeks of 2001, our white-gloved events team hoisted the faded, 10-by-12-foot banner, which had witnessed the passage of Lincoln's cortege, for a dozen or so displays in a new moment of a nation's passage. I thought it lent the right note of sobriety and hope, and as I delivered my remarks to our employees in my post-9/11 holiday party speeches, I spoke with an emotion that I felt more deeply than ever before in any of these gatherings.

I can't remember exactly what I said, or how I said it, only something that went along the lines of: We don't know what the future holds. Our backs are to the wall, but we've been there before, and we've always pulled through. As long as the Men's Wearhouse, and the nation, sticks to our principles and values, we will make it through this crisis.

Maybe I overdid it with the clichés, but the feeling—the intent—is what really mattered, and I meant every word of it, as sincerely as the bond I had forged with our customers when I told them over and over again, "I guarantee it."

Like so many other things in my life, the speech, the flag, the mood, the reaction—everything—came together somewhat unconsciously. My gut told me that this was time for a paradigm shift, a time for inspiration rather than motivation, a time for me as a leader to bring our rank and file into a state of coherence in response to a national crisis.

Ben Zaricor gave me the visual tool for the job, an old flag that represented another era that had been championed by the truest hero of the American experience, the president who presided over the greatest paradigm shift in our nation's history—the beginning of our transition out of slavery.

• • •

I don't know about most people, but I've found that looking back over my life and examining some of the things that I did, some of the crucial decisions I made—much of the impulse that drove me, it all pretty much came out of nowhere. I did have a vague notion of wanting to start my own business, even if I hadn't planned for it to be in men's tailored retail clothing. I did want to run a business in the spirit of the sixties, but I didn't have the slightest clue at the time that the one I created would be on the front edge of stakeholder capitalism.

No doubt, I'd been raised right, by ethical people who modeled and taught me the ideals of hard work, integrity, and responsibility, and how you have to do it all with a sense of fun (thanks, Nana Jessie, for the lessons in chocolate ice cream). I'd always had an intuitive understanding of the Golden Rule—it wasn't an abstract concept to me. My sixties experiences hardened my value system, and that would underlie the business I created: we had to make money, of course, but it didn't have to be at the expense of everybody else. We wanted to succeed, but we wanted to bring others along in our success—our customers, our communities.

Right there in our mission statement, which I wrote on the back of the cocktail napkin after it looked like we'd made it past the early hurdles, it said that we wanted to enhance the community, that we wanted to become, as a company, self-actualized people. I'd seen how business could be corrupted, and the Foley's experience with the canary-yellow sport coats triggered an unconscious, unformed idea—an impulse—about how to do it right.

Eventually, this unconscious evolution of my thinking toward what I came to know as stakeholder capitalism became more and more of a formalized concept. If I had to put a date on when it really crystallized for me, I'd say it was shortly after we went public with the Men's Wearhouse, when I read the book *Real Magic* by the inspirational, motivational author, Wayne Dyer. What really struck me was Dyer's argument that in many instances—in business, in sports, in life—you first have to *believe* in something before you can actually *see* it become a reality. The reversal of the standard line "I'll believe it when I see it" was a major paradigm shift, one that absolutely blew me away. It told me that belief, although not absolute, precedes material reality.

The idea hit me right between the eyes, probably because it was the opposite of the advice I got growing up.

I was generally a pretty good kid. I know my parents were mostly happy with me. But there were occasions when I fell short of parental expectations, didn't put out maximum effort on a school paper, or wasn't on top of things with the collections on the paper route. In cases like these, I promised my parents that I would work harder and do better. I almost always did. But no matter the circumstance, my father would almost always end the conversation on a gentle but challenging note. He'd hit me with that skeptical idiom, "I'll believe it when I see it."

The Wayne Dyer book flipped my father's adage entirely on its head. It also stirred an entire paradigm shift in my thinking, one that pried my brain

wide open and allowed me to challenge convention. Maybe it wasn't best, as
Machiavelli wrote, for leaders to rule out of fear rather than inspire out of
love. Maybe you had to believe, like Dyer said, before you could see.

And when it came to running a public company, it was around the time
that I first read Wayne Dyer's book that I began to see that business, if it
was going to take responsibility for the whole of society, would have to take
a paradigm shift away from the prevailing doctrine of maximizing shareholder value.

• • •

In addition to reading some influential books, it took decades of experience
for my understanding of stakeholder capitalism to take a firmer and formalized hold. Witnessing the hard work of my father. The will to do good
for others exemplified by my mother. The lessons on integrity from Papa
George. The wink of approval and the idea of fun that I gained from Nana
Jessie. The overriding importance of idealism and progressive politics from
my college years. The ragtag teamwork that created the Men's Wearhouse.
It all kind of mashed up into something that I'd never really sought to label,
until the idea of stakeholder capitalism came into my life.

Whatever you believe, you can ultimately see.

That bad experience with Foley's had turned out to be formative. I just
knew, on that drive home from Houston to Dallas, that there had to be a
better way to do business. There had to be something better than being able
to screw over anybody you want and not think twice about it. Did a business
have to keep everything for itself and leave nothing for anybody else? Was
that the unalterable logic of capitalism? Was that the only way it could end
when you ordered a bunch of ridiculously ugly canary-yellow sport coats?
To chop them up, demand that the rookie road man take them back, and
then stiff the poor bastard when he comes around again to make a sale?

As an antiwar protester in the sixties, I never believed, like some of my
fellow activists, that capitalism must lead to imperialist domination in places
like Vietnam. And as a businessman starting up my own company, I never
believed that capitalism means you have to exploit everything around you
in the service of maximized shareholder value. Creating my own company
gave me the chance to do things differently, based on values instilled in me
from the beginning and polished with the veneer of a progressive time in

which I came into my own. The hippie in me told me there had to be a better way, that there had to be something else, that running a company didn't mean you had to bow down to the altar of profit and submit every other component of your person to its maximization. As I learned through my association with the World Business Academy, a socially conscious company had an obligation to look out for everybody. We had to train and treat our employees right. We had to deal with our suppliers fairly. We had to be good neighbors. We had to provide the best product with the best service at the best price, and if that meant that the stock price or our bottom line had to take a little bit of a haircut, then hand me the scissors. I made that guarantee to myself, our employees, our suppliers, and our customers.

For a businessman whose company was being traded on the open market, this type of a belief system represented a shift in the working paradigm of capitalism. It flew directly in the face of the first principles of Milton Friedman.

Personally, I've got nothing against shareholders. Hell, I'm one myself. But to base an entire economic structure on satisfying the whims of people who own your stock or who are thinking about buying it? It's just not sustainable for the whole of society—that World Business Academy concept again. If the only thing that manufacturers worry about is maximizing profits, they'll burn the Amazon. After all, they'd be doing the most logical thing of shareholder capitalism—maximizing their profits.

Unfortunately, unless you're Jesus, or the Buddha, or Moses, or any of the great spiritual beings, you're probably going to have to start out in business as a lout, a bully, a dominator, a classic Type A alpha male. At least that's the way it's set up in our prevailing Darwinian economic reality. Sometimes you've got to be something of an asshole to get your idea off the ground. Nobody except family and frat brothers and maybe a vendor who has a stake in your success is going to help you. When the choice is between your survival and your ethics, it's not much of a choice. If you survive, and if you thrive, then the time will come when ethics and social responsibility *must* enter into the conversation.

I'd like to think that we at the Men's Wearhouse were a little better than most. From the beginning, we paid our people a little better. We saw the value of racial and gender diversity. We wanted to fit into our community, and we damn sure weren't going to abuse our suppliers the way Foley's did. We were tough competitors, and I did everything that I had to do to make sure that we survived. We did make it through, thanks to the wild success of our TV ads, and we were able to move beyond the fear of failure that can drive companies into decisions that certainly don't benefit the whole of society.

I'd achieved a modicum of wealth. I'd proven myself to my father, and now, I thought, it was time to live up to the spirit of my mother. I threw in with the World Business Academy in 1987. I read Wayne Dyer and Willis Harman and Michael Ray.

I think it was 1995 when I met Whole Foods Market cofounder and CEO John Mackey at a Bear Stearns luncheon. (Nearly twenty years later, Mackey and coauthor Raj Sisodia would publish their seminal *Conscious Capitalism*, the 2014 work that still lays out the precepts of stakeholder capitalism as well as any other treatise on the subject.) At the luncheon, Mackey and I joked about trading our companies, Whole Foods for the Men's Wearhouse, straight up. More seriously, the two of us talked about trying to manage companies that worked for the benefit of everybody, not just the shareholder, even though I don't remember either of us using the specific term "stakeholder capitalism" in our conversation.

When his book came out a couple of decades later, after I got fired, I remember thinking to myself, "Holy shit. We did this stuff at the Men's Wearhouse for forty years!"

Only I was too frantic at the time to put a label on it. All I knew is that we were building the strength of our company one store at a time while we unconsciously looked out for our customers and employees as well as our stockholders. If you ask me, I'd say we were right up there at the forefront of the stakeholder movement with companies such as Whole Foods, Southwest Airlines, Patagonia, and even Starbucks.

The thing is, they all stuck with it and thrived. Me, I got thrown out by the forces of greed, of the shareholder mindset, and my ousters have since gone bankrupt.

As for stakeholder capitalism, there is no big mystery about it. All it says is that workers, vendors, customers, and communities should be held in the same regard as stockholders when a business makes its decisions. At the Men's Wearhouse, our unarticulated version of stakeholder capitalism meant more than just not burning down the rain forest. I had made the commitment after my Foley's experience that I was going to treat everybody with dignity, and that every decision I made I was going to consider the impact on the whole of society—not just the bottom line, but something where everybody can win. You could see it in our mission statement. As we got closer to our IPO, I knew that the more voices we listened to, the more we all could come to peace with our intuitive selves.

By the time we transferred to the New York Stock Exchange, I was the CEO of a company that at the beginning of the new millennium sold $1.33 billion worth of suits and slacks and other items of men's apparel out of 651 stores in the United States and Canada, turning a profit of $84.7 million. We were no longer an adult lemonade stand. We had become a mature, successful company with executives and distribution centers and our own private jet, which once flew me from Oakland to Chicago to pick up an award and give a five-minute speech before flying me home as soon as I finished. We also had our mission: to empower everybody in the organization to make decisions on the spot, without fear that if they screwed it up, they'd get reamed. It meant the top guy—me—communicating with everybody face-to-face, and I did it with thousands of people. I hated memos, and wasn't very fond of emails, texts—stuff gets lost in the translation from your fingers to the keyboard. You've got to talk to your people. It meant constant experimentation. Try something. If it works, great. If it doesn't, try something else. Mistakes are good. They are great teachers. We all learned from them. It meant leading out of love instead of fear. It meant inspiring as well as motivating people.

It meant sacrificing the marginal benefit of an executive or a shareholder, to the betterment of all. It meant taking everything into consideration when you make a decision rather than just the bottom line, which often means a theoretical race to the bottom.

It meant seeing the public as our partner and not building a business model based on taking advantage of the consumer.

It meant hiring people full time, paying them benefits, and putting everyone in an employee stock ownership program. Karl Marx may have taken up painting instead of writing if they had ESOPs in 1848.

It meant not getting obscenely rich at the expense of everybody else in the company. My base salary never exceeded $600,000, and never rose to more than twelve times the pay of our average store manager.

It meant that when you caught an employee stealing, you didn't automatically fire him or her. It meant finding out what was going on in that person's life, working with them, and maybe giving them a second chance.

Sometimes at the Men's Wearhouse, former thieves turned into valuable and loyal employees. It meant no drug tests or criminal background checks on our employees, unless they had jobs like drivers where the law required it.

It meant rejection of the idea that we were in business for the primary purpose of maximizing shareholder value.

From its inception, capitalism has rightfully come under an honest and brutal critique. But it's also important to understand that capitalism does not necessarily have to produce a Gilded Age, or the massive income inequality that has taken hold in America the past forty years. If they embrace the values of the stakeholder concept, capitalism and its companies can do good, no matter their size.

In my years at the Men's Wearhouse, I was all about wealth creation and the accumulation of capital. Like I said, I think Adam Smith got it right when he wrote *The Wealth of Nations* in 1776. And he got it even more right seventeen years earlier, in 1759, when he published *The Theory of Moral Sentiments*, his work on the moral underpinning of a just society that's artic-ulated best in stakeholder capitalism.

• • •

As a kid, I went to synagogue mostly because my parents made me. When I got old enough to make my own choice, I stopped. I loved the traditions of the Jewish religion, especially Passover, and I always maintained at least a flicker of a spiritual flame. I just didn't want to get all religious over it. Spirit, I thought, was something else, and I've always considered myself spiritual, although I certainly never tended to my spiritual side in public. Until I got a phone call out of nowhere from the late Winston "Wink" Franklin, presi-dent of the Institute of Noetic Sciences—IONS, the insiders called it.

The institute was founded in 1973—same year as the Men's Wearhouse—by Dr. Edgar Mitchell, the sixth man to walk on the moon. On his return from the Apollo 14 mission, Mitchell underwent a spiritually transformative experience that I can't even begin to understand, observing, through the windshield of his space capsule, a blue Earth floating against a galactic backdrop. A scientist by training, he felt that the scientific method fell short when it came to explaining the sense of universal connectedness he felt on his return to Earth. In his search for an explanation, Dr. Mitchell established the institute.

Once I joined the institute and became a major donor, Dr. Mitchell gave me a plaque containing a small American flag that he packed along with him on his moon shot. It is inscribed, "As a fellow explorer, I present you with this flag that I carried to the moon on the Apollo 14 Mission, February 1971." It's definitely a keeper, and I have it proudly displayed in my dining room.

Dr. Mitchell's legacy has since been colored by his expressed belief in the existence of UFOs. Believe what you want about that, though in April 2020 the United States Navy revealed it has observed something that looks very much like alien aircraft. It's a pretty big universe out there.

I don't know how Wink got on to me. Maybe he saw me guaranteeing things on television. Maybe he checked me out through the World Business Academy and liked the idea of entrepreneurs stepping up to take responsibility for the fractured planet. Or it could be that he just spotted me as a potential donor.

"George," Wink told me in that first call, which must have been in the late nineties, from his headquarters in Sausalito, "I just have an *intuitive* feeling you're going to be interested in this."

I did a little research on Wink and IONS, and I discovered that "intuitive" described what his organization was all about, in a single word. Turned out Wink was right. I was immediately interested.

I saw noetics as another example of a paradigm shift, *from* the bifurcation of knowledge and belief, *to* their interrelatedness. A great leap of faith leads to the hypothesis that begins a scientific validation. Intuition spawns inquiry.

This intuition thing had always intrigued me. I wanted to know more about it, where it came from, and what it was, other than knowing something without the benefit of seeing, hearing, smelling, tasting, or touching it. According to IONS, intuition tunes you in to a deeper sense of knowledge, beyond the five senses, or what might get lost in your senses' interpretation of reality.

Intuition is what makes you take a great leap, like discovering gravity, or knowing that if you sell suits without the Nino Cerruti label for a hundred dollars less than the competition, you can succeed in the men's clothing industry.

From the beginning, we ran the Men's Wearhouse mostly on instinct. Like many great businesses, it was born on an intuitive impulse. Nobody handed us a blueprint that said "here's how you sell clothes to men." Nobody had done any studies on the subject.

Little did I know, there actually was a group of scientists studying such leaps of the unconscious. Wink's organization had been conducting experiments on the subject for nearly thirty years. His institute sought out scientific explanations on things like human innovation, publishing peer-reviewed papers on efforts to verify the ineffable.

I understood noetics to represent the meeting ground—the intersection—between science and spirit. While philosophers such as Descartes saw nothing mutually contradictory between the two, the scientists at IONS searched for evidence to show that the two actually are *complementary*. Scientists and priests *can* sit at the same table.

The institute seemed like a good place for me to examine my own concept of intuition, and I did give Wink Franklin some money, and he put me on the IONS board. The deeper I dove into the workings of IONS, the more it hit me that this was the intellectual application of what we did from the days of the adult lemonade stand.

Given my background at the World Business Academy, I wondered if maybe businesspeople—acting for the benefit of the whole society—might belong at the same table as the priests and scientists, envisioning a world where all stakeholders' interests are taken into account. It shouldn't have surprised me when I discovered that Willis Harman, one of the cofounders of the World Business Academy, had been president of IONS for nearly twenty years before he died in 1997.

I found myself fascinated by the group's effort to explain, at the intersection of science and spirit, that which defies the limited explanation of the rational mind.

• • •

In the New Year of 2002, after the disaster of the previous September's terrorist attacks, America regained its footing, and the Men's Wearhouse followed. Our growth had slowed from its stratospheric rise in the nineties but could still only be described as inexorable. Our size and spread helped us weather the storm of the terrorist attacks, and five other economic downturns in the first thirty-five years of our existence. Our early move into technology, our training programs, our terrific relationships with our growing number of suppliers, our faith in our employees, our belief in our customers—we were creating a model for what a stakeholder operation ought to look like.

We tried new things, like tuxedo rentals. We gave dry cleaning a shot, and we had as many as twenty-four stores up and running in the Houston area by the end of 2004. We offered our own credit card.

We looked to make some inroads with a new generation of shoppers who had *really* turned their backs on not just suits and ties but slacks and button-down shirts and pretty much anything that you could have previously characterized as conventional. In 2008, we signed a deal with Ultimate Fighting Championship star Randy Couture to carry his new clothing lines for men and women. This was all about patterned T-shirts, hoodies, ripped and faded blue jeans, denim, leather and camo jackets, shorts, tanks, bikinis—you name it, as long as it was tight and flashed skin. I never thought I'd be so into frayed jeans.

Randy and I produced a four-minute heavy-metal training video, ending with a coordinated fist pump and the promise of, "We guarantee it."

We played off guitar virtuoso Stevie Ray Vaughan's biggest hit with a women's wedding fashion line we called Bride and Joy. We brought in Joseph Abboud as our chief creative director and carried the renowned designer's latest works exclusively.

We survived the 2008 stock market crash and the Great Recession that followed, to grow into a chain of 1,143 stores in the United States and Canada that did an annual $2.5 billion in sales and generated $198 million in profits in 2012, and made the *Fortune* "100 Best Companies To Work For" list twelve times in fifteen years.

As we became more and more successful, I came to better understand the impulses that impacted my worldview. I allowed them to inform my actions. I turned my beliefs into visions. I acted on them, not being quite sure what would happen. I mystified some of the people around me and pissed off others who dismissed theories without empirical explanations as gibberish. Some people humored me. Some people talked trash about me behind my back. Some people told me to my face, "George, you don't know what the fuck you're talking about." Maybe not. But I do know how we built the Men's Wearhouse.

A long time ago, we decided that our shareholders would make a little less money, that our growth rates and market capitalization would be a little lower, so that all of the company's employees, all of its customers, all of its suppliers, its entire community, would all be a little better off.

In 2020, some 181 CEOs of the biggest companies in the world signed on to the Business Roundtable "Statement on the Purpose of a Corporation," saying that they share "a fundamental commitment to all of our stakeholders" in their actions. I guess that makes them all stakeholder capitalists, at least in their own minds, although—just like my father—I'd have to see it to believe it with most of them. We are, after all, talking about the world's biggest banks, oil companies, and pharmaceutical companies.

Still, I'd say that's what you call a paradigm shift.

→ 8 ←

Pot Luck

The time was early 1996. The place was the Men's Wearhouse retreat at Pajaro Dunes, on Monterey Bay. And the occasion was the first and last meeting of the DEA—the Dunes Entertainment Authority.

On the agenda, only one item: the status of the upcoming campaign to legalize the use of medicinal marijuana in the state of California. It was *our* DEA's top priority, in our war against the war on drugs.

Steve Kubby, the well-known marijuana activist, was on hand. So was Marsha Rosenbaum, a principle investigator for the National Institute on Drug Abuse. Also in attendance were my ex-wife, Lorri; pot luminaries such as husband and wife writers and activists Chris Conrad and Mikki Norris; and a few others, including the former San Francisco supervisor and my long-time political advisor, Jim Gonzalez.

At some point I called Ethan Nadelmann, the founder of the Lindesmith Center in New York City. Ethan acted as the US surrogate for multibillionaire financier George Soros to reform the draconian drug laws in the United States, among other harm-reduction initiatives. We also rang up Bill Zimmerman, another leading political consultant, like my man Jim. Over the last thirty years, Bill had been all over the country, organizing for the civil rights movement in the South and against the war in Vietnam. He managed Tom Hayden's campaign for a US Senate seat in California in 1976 and helped get Harold Washington elected as Chicago's first Black mayor in 1983.

We convened at the Dunes mainly to see what we could do to revive the sputtering medicinal marijuana campaign begun in the 1980s by Dennis Peron, who promoted pot as a salve for the AIDS crisis that was then ravaging the gay community in San Francisco. In 1991, he qualified a medical marijuana initiative for the city ballot, and it won with 79 percent of the vote. Taking the medical pot concept statewide, Dennis organized a volunteer signature-gathering effort to place such an initiative on the '96 general-election ballot. This time, things weren't working out so well. By the time we met at the Dunes, he'd only collected ninety thousand signatures. We needed six hundred thousand to qualify, and we only had five more weeks to get them.

Ethan gave us the cold, hard analysis on the speakerphone. This campaign was going to die, he told us, unless we came up with some very big money very fast to hire professional signature-gathering firms, which paid street hustlers a buck or so for every valid signature they could get from registered voters. Ethan estimated the cost for such a campaign at $2 million: $1 million for signatures and $1 million for television advertising. And he told us that we needed it, like, right now. Otherwise, it was going to be "wait until next year," or the year after that. But in 1996, with Bill Clinton running for reelection and medical marijuana polling very well in what looked to be a high-turnout campaign, we all knew that our time had to be now.

We all had the highest hopes for Dennis. We really wanted his volunteer effort to do the trick. It was a nice hope, and a nice try, but it was a fantasy. The reality was that California politics had become such that if you wanted to qualify a ballot measure in a limited time frame, you had to go with the pros. You had to hire the firms that could get people to sign petitions on whatever issue and whatever side of any issue that you could imagine, whether it was saving the whales, or killing the mountain lions, or making it harder to vaccinate the young, or easier to euthanize the old and sick, or legalizing the use of medical marijuana by anyone with a doctor's recommendation.

We all got that. Only the price tag made us gulp.

As George Soros's point man, Nadelmann had access to big money. Soros had shocked the world financial markets four years earlier when he made a billion dollars in a day as a hedge fund manager who hedged against the British pound. By the time we gathered at the Dunes, Mr. Soros's net worth had increased to $2.5 billion.

"George," Ethan told me in the telephone call, while the group of about a dozen people listened in, "I think I can get five hundred thousand from George Soros."

Ethan went on to say that there also was a high probability that he could lean on John Sperling, my friend who founded the University of Phoenix, for $500,000, and that he could persuade Peter B. Lewis, the founder and president of Progressive Insurance in Cleveland, to contribute another half million. Unfortunately, Ethan said, none of those guys, including Soros, were likely to jump in unless California showed that it was willing to put some skin in the game, too. By California, I took it that Ethan meant me, which would entail some risk on my part. As the CEO of a publicly traded company, I still hadn't come out of the closet as a pot smoker.

All I needed to do, Ethan said, was contribute the first $500,000 as "the California guy" to get this done. Then, Soros, Sperling, and Lewis would make the leap. "Otherwise," he said, "these guys won't think we're serious."

It was a pretty big number, $500,000. Soros, Sperling, and Lewis—they were all billionaires. For me, the five hundred large amounted to five-sixths of my annual salary. I'd have to cash in some of my stock in the Men's Wearhouse. Like about 38,500 shares worth.

I needed about a second to conclude my deliberations. I told Ethan I was good for the money.

Soros, Sperling, and Lewis quickly came across with their share of the political freight, and they're the ones who got all the press that year as the great funders of Proposition 215, the medical marijuana initiative. Which was just fine with me. I sure didn't want the publicity, and I asked the team to please keep my name out of the press releases. If somebody looked me up in the public records as a major donor, fine. I just didn't need to go out asking for trouble. The bottom line was, the signature-gathering effort saved the campaign and got us on the ballot, and a very strong 56 percent of California voters responded by voting in favor of the measure.

With Proposition 215, California became the first state in the nation to legalize marijuana in any form. We made history—against the drug war, in the nascent marijuana legalization movement that has swept across the country ever since. Now, it looks like it won't stop until all fifty states and the federal government enact their own versions of legalization, both recreational (now on the books in sixteen states, including California and the District of Columbia) and medicinal (enacted everywhere else except Alabama, if you include cannabidiol products that don't get you high), with assorted levels of decriminalization in two other states.

When it comes to weed, it looks like America has finally come to its senses. After more than a half century of ridiculous and mendacious opposition to marijuana that has always been hysterical and that at times has bordered on comical, everybody appears to be coming to the realization that, in the end, pot really isn't that big of a deal.

• • •

I first started smoking pot in spring semester of my freshman year in college, which makes it about fifty-three years now that I've enjoyed the herb. These days, I like pot just as much as I ever have, although on the days that, for whatever reason, I don't smoke it, I don't miss it.

You know what I like the most about pot?

It brings me *down.*

It took me a couple of years as head of the Men's Wearhouse to realize there's a part of me that's certified alpha male. Maybe the term isn't typically associated with guys who played bridge in high school, but I played the game as seriously as Ray Lewis used to play middle linebacker for the Baltimore Ravens. And once I got the company up and running, I competed as hard as anybody in business, although I was more into win-win than just win.

Type As sometimes need a little respite, to stop taking themselves so seriously. In my own case, I think that might be the main reason I get high. I love to be able to lose that edge of intensity. Otherwise my head might blow off, of its own accord.

Take golf, for instance. When I'm out on the golf course and smoking a joint, nothing can go wrong. Out there, my competitive urges tend to flow, and I need to calm them down. I hit a bad shot when I'm straight, and forget about it—I beat the hell out of myself. My surliness rubs off on everyone around me. It ruins the day. But when I take a puff and I hit a bad shot, it's like, so what?

I think pot actually improves my game. It helps me get in the groove. I'm not encumbered by extraneous thought. I get into the feel of the swing rather than parsing it down to a microanalytical level. The business world can wait. I'm less tough on myself.

Being stoned relaxes me. Being relaxed eases my mind, opening it up to new ideas, new creative possibilities. When I'm high, I keep a notepad close at hand, to document the good ideas that dance into my head before they dance out. At the Men's Wearhouse, pot helped me through patches of stress. Whenever I had to give a talk in public, if I tensed up during preparation, I eased it with a hit off a joint. Lots of times, if I had to give a speech on a Tuesday, I'd prepare on Sunday while watching a football or baseball game on TV, notepad open, pen in my hand, and a rolled joint sitting in the ashtray on the end table, ready to be lit. On my game day, when it came time to give my talk, sometimes I'd first have a smoke.

Let me be clear: I don't recommend pot for everybody. It's up to each to make their own choice. As a Type A, the marijuana flower softens me up. But if you're already relaxed, pot may not be the right intoxicant for you. You're probably better off with a drink. Have a glass of wine, a beer, or scotch, which I used to enjoy, until I quit drinking forty years ago because it was bad for *me*. This is not science, of course. It's just my observation, based on a lifetime of experiments within the laboratory of myself. Get an alpha male liquored up and put him behind the wheel of a car and he thinks he's Mario Andretti. Give him a puff of cannabis and he's far more likely to obey the speed limit. Pot does affect everybody differently, according to the real experts. Taking my own personal inventory, I can tell you this: it has not impaired me physically or mentally in the slightest. I am finding out now, at age seventy-two, that I do get tired easier when I smoke pot. But I'm not sure if that is a function of the pot or my advancing age.

• • •

From the time I took my first hit off my first joint, I've been a marijuana advocate. Advocate, yes. Activist, no, until the 1996 California medical marijuana campaign, when my $500,000 contribution established my public pot persona.

I didn't ask for it, and neither did I fight it. The people in my life who smoked pot knew me for a pot smoker. The people in my life who didn't smoke pot didn't have a clue. If word did leak out a little prior to 1996, I didn't pay much attention to it, or to what people said or thought about my personal practices. Same as everything else about pot, it wasn't that big of a deal.

Then I made a little mistake, one that instructed me to keep an eye on myself. My blunder occurred after one of those excellent Bridge School concerts, the benefits that Neil and Pegi Young put on every year to raise money for the Bay Area educational program for kids with physical and speech impairments. Neil, of course, headlined the shows at the Shoreline Amphitheatre in Mountain View, over marquees that included the likes of Bruce Springsteen, Tom Petty, Bob Dylan, and Elton John. It should come as no surprise that I enhanced my enjoyment of the concerts by joining the thousands of others getting high. No big deal, I thought, if I smoked a joint in public. I never stopped to consider how it might affect the image of the Men's Wearhouse, until I got a voice mail the day after one of the shows: somebody apparently took major offense at my momentary indulgence. "I saw what you were doing last night at the show," the caller said, "and I'm never going to shop in any of your stores ever again."

Most definitely, it was a failure on my part to forget that whether I liked it not, I was a public figure. The call made me realize that I had to be more responsible, that I was the well-established "I Guarantee It" guy whose face flashed into millions of people's living rooms every night. The success of my business depended, in no small degree, on my good reputation. Even if I love pot and how it helps me live my life, and am revulsed by the excesses of the war on drugs, I know that pot can cause trouble for certain people, and I don't want to contribute to anyone's pain. I am first and foremost into harm reduction.

I knew, and I know, a lot of people in the sports, business, and entertainment worlds who smoked pot and benefited from it. I've been more up-front with my usage than most, and, since my forced departure from the Men's Wearhouse, I've come to appreciate the recognition. But that call the day after the Bridge Concert alerted me to my personal, as well as corporate, responsibilities. So I dialed it down a little bit.

At the next year's Bridge Concert, when I felt like a smoke, I went backstage.

• • •

Of all the interesting people I've gotten high with, there is one experience with one man that I will always cherish. Consciousness instigator Baba Ram Dass had already had a stroke by the time I met him at his Marin County home sometime in the early 2000s. This was a good forty years after Ram Dass, then Richard Alpert, partnered with fellow Harvard professor Timothy Leary in the early sixties in their experiments that popularized the use of LSD and other psychedelics as stimulators of mystical experience. It was also decades after Alpert took his spiritual journey to India, received a new name from his guru, and returned to America to write his bestselling book *Be Here Now* about his life's path toward higher consciousness and spiritual salvation.

I went to meet Ram Dass at his house in San Anselmo with my friend Chuck Blitz, the progressive Santa Barbara real estate developer and philanthropist, who made the introduction. The three of us and another friend of Chuck's sat with Ram Dass in his living room, talking about politics and business and—our favorite subject—consciousness. In the course of the discussion, I asked Ram Dass if he would mind if I rolled a joint. No problem, he said. I did my thing with the papers and the pot, lit it, and after I took a hit, I offered it to Ram Dass, mainly out of politeness. I thought he'd given up all drugs at this point in his life. To my surprise, he accepted the joint, and he and I smoked it down to about nothing. Naturally, I rolled another, and we smoked that one, too, and I rolled another, and then three more, and Ram Dass and I smoked all six of them, in a span of less than two hours, while the four of us talked about everything from the profound to the mundane, the latter of which included an analysis of the presidency of George W. Bush.

It truly was one of the most remarkable experiences of my life, getting high with this iconic figure of science and spirit. One thing will forever be embedded in my memory of Ram Dass, and that was how clear his eyes were, even though we'd been smoking pot for two hours. I'll also never forget his salutation as we prepared to leave.

"George," Ram Dass said to me, "I don't want you ever to think that any of the politicos or intellectuals out there are making a bigger contribution than you are. What you are doing at the Men's Wearhouse dwarfs anything we are doing."

I know my recollection of his words rings of vanity, but I don't share them to shower myself with excessive praise. This validation that I (a businessman, a guy who used to sell canary-yellow sport coats out of the trunk of my Buick, who made a couple of moves in the garment trade that paid off), by including my employees, my suppliers, my customers, and the whole of society at the forefront of my thinking, was making a difference—it meant the world to me. I accepted Ram Dass's affirmation that personally and professionally I was on a good path. It was a blessing, from one of the great spirits of my lifetime—consecrated by an herb that, in that moment, served as a sacrament.

· · ·

As for other drugs, I was just never that interested. In most cases, I just didn't really feel the need. I didn't get much of a kick from cocaine and only used it once or twice. I liked ecstasy plenty, but that's not something you want to do every day. I never got into downers. They didn't match my personality type. And alcohol and me, we just didn't agree.

I don't think I've ever been more embarrassed than the time I got kicked out of Game 6 of the NBA Finals in Houston in 1981. We had season tickets on the floor at The Summit, the arena where the hometown Rockets were down 3–2 to the Boston Celtics in the championship series. The Rockets fell way behind early in the game but were making a big run in the closing minutes when the referees whistled them for a foul on a crucial possession. Drunk and obviously out of control, I stormed out of my seat in protest and onto the playing floor. The security people rightfully escorted me out of the arena. I'm lucky I didn't get arrested. This is something I would never come close to doing after smoking a joint, which helps me to just kick back and enjoy the spirit of the athletic competition.

Just a few weeks later, I had another very close and serious call with the law, one that served as a wake-up call. I'd had a few drinks and was probably driving above the legal limit when the Houston cops pulled me over. The officers knew I was drunk, but I was able to talk my way out of a DUI, with a promise to the police that I would call my brother and have him drive me home. Jimmy came and got me. He was none too happy about it, and neither was I.

Those two incidents, occurring just a matter of days from each other, alerted me to my problem with booze. They were just two examples of many ugly and crazy occurrences of mood and behavior of mine that I associated with the bottle. It was an addiction that ran in the family, I guess, certainly through my mother, who was a hard-core alcoholic.

I took my last drink not long after the basketball game and the encounter with the Houston cop. I was in San Francisco, with the woman who would become my first wife, at the bar of the St. Francis Hotel. I can't remember what she ordered, but I went with my usual—scotch on the rocks. When it came, I told her, "This is going to be my last drink." Thirty-nine years later, I still haven't had another.

The next day, I checked into a thirty-day rehab program. I lasted three weeks. I bailed when my fiancée came up to visit me and I asked if I could take her out to dinner in Santa Rosa. My counselor—I'm sure he was at least nineteen years old—told me I couldn't go. I asked him why not, and he said, "Because you'll have a drink." I told him, "No, I won't." He disagreed, and I was gone. As I left, the counselor said, "If you drive down that hill, don't come back." Well, I did come back, and I resumed the program, and a few days later I asked the same counselor if there was any place on the premises where I could go and peacefully smoke a joint without bothering any of the other clients. He told me I couldn't smoke pot in rehab. I was okay with the rule, but it gave me no choice but to thank him and the treatment center for their time before I left for good. I rode off into what is still an alcohol-free life. Nothing inherently wrong with the stuff. It just isn't for me.

I hear a lot from people I know who are into Alcoholics Anonymous, and who have benefited greatly from the program. They all talk about how you have to hit your bottom before you come back up. I respectfully disagree. I tell them, "When you're drinking, you're on an elevator going down, but you can get off on any floor."

Pot helped me get off the elevator. If I'm going to be addicted to anything, better that it be to the substance that does the least harm.

• • •

Maybe the most bald-faced political lie ever perpetrated on the American public was the one that began in the 1930s under Harry J. Anslinger, President Herbert Hoover's appointee to run the Treasury Department's Federal Bureau of Narcotics. Anslinger and the government conspired with the crackpot film producer Dwain Esper to create the outrageous, hilarious, mendacious movie *Reefer Madness*. By the time I reached dope-smoking age, the epic 1936 film that depicted teenagers becoming insane and immoral while experimenting with the evil weed rivaled old Marx Brothers movies as the funniest thing to watch while stoned. Decades before Nancy Reagan implored us to "just say no," the scare tactics of the Anslinger-Esper media campaign launched the first official governmental iteration of the war on drugs.

"These high school boys and girls are having a hop at the local soda fountain," the narrator intones in the madness of the *Reefer Madness* trailer. "Innocently, they dance: innocent of a new and deadly menace lurking behind closed doors—marijuana, the burning weed with its roots in hell."

Teenagers jump out of windows. Wild men pound mad rhythms on the piano. Middle-aged men lure kids to their destruction. "Smoking the soul-destroying reefer, they find a moment's pleasure, but at a terrible price: debauchery, violence, murder. Suicide!" the narrator says.

Funny as they are, films like this, and the policies they propagandized, always pissed me off more than they amused me. By the 1980s, the war on drugs motivated me to launch a counteroffensive. Though our country's backward approach to drugs goes at least as far back as Prohibition, the moment that I can clearly remember thinking they took things too far began with the 1988 creation of the Office of National Drug Control Policy, and the "three strikes" law that came with it. According to the idea of "three strikes," young men—disproportionately African American—could be imprisoned for twenty-five to life for "crimes" as insignificant as possession of marijuana. I saw this whole system taking shape and knew, as an avid pot smoker, that weed was nowhere near dangerous enough to put someone caught with it in jail for a lifetime.

I shared my fears with similarly outraged entrepreneurs, artists, writers, politicians, academics, scientists, and everyday people. Like many, I was indignant about the leaders of the "drug war" trying to impose their preferences about how to get high on the country. I didn't see them cracking down on booze, even though it can be incredibly dangerous, especially compared to the effects of pot. I thought back to my visions of cops during my college days looking to crack you over the head while they cracked down on pot. I began, like many others, to think that maybe one way to undercut the conflict would be the legalization of all drugs. Marijuana to start.

Toward the end of 1995, I had the good fortune to attend the first State of the World Forum, which was held in San Francisco. Former Soviet president Mikhail Gorbachev, in the first half decade after the end of the Cold War, organized the conference to gather some of the leading thinkers in the world to think and talk about its biggest problems. It must have been at the session entitled "Creative Approaches to the Drug Crisis" where I met some of the people who, like me, had had enough of the drug war, especially as it pertained to pot. I believe that's when I first started talking to Ethan Nadelmann, Dennis Peron, Steve Kubby, Chris Conrad, and others about launching a medical marijuana initiative. I invited them to Pajaro Dunes for several weekend retreats, including the one at which we created our very own DEA, on the night I made the $500,000 commitment that led to the matching contributions from George Soros, John Sperling, and Peter B. Lewis.

Once we qualified Proposition 215 for the ballot, I backed away and let our political guys, Jim Gonzalez and Bill Zimmerman, do their jobs. They performed to perfection, holding off the more militant in our movement from antagonizing the public with a high-profile, in-your-face campaign. Jim and Bill's plan was to lay low until the last two weeks before voting, and then bust loose with an intense and highly personal advertising campaign in which the face of our movement wouldn't be somebody out of Haight-Ashbury. Instead, we featured an oncologist, a woman with breast cancer, and a nurse who snuck pot to her cancer-stricken husband, which she credited with buying him two more years of life beyond what his doctors predicted. We never mentioned marijuana without first inserting the word "medical" in front of it. I trusted our team, and it turned out that they were right.

Medicinal marijuana, and then the flat-out legalization campaigns, have since taken hold across the country. I'm proud that Proposition 215 ignited the movement.

I haven't really done a whole lot since then as far as public participation in the nationwide marijuana movement. I did give a major donation to a 2010 campaign to legalize recreational pot use in California. That measure failed, but the genie had already been let out of the bottle with Proposition 215. Colorado and Washington passed recreational use laws, and nobody saw any teenagers jumping out of windows à la *Reefer Madness*, at least to any increased extent. California voters passed a recreational legalization measure in 2016, Proposition 64—the Adult Use of Marijuana Act, which allows for recreational pot use by anybody over the age of twenty-one and has made it possible for me to satisfy my reefer madness by having the herb delivered directly to my front door. I endorsed Proposition 64, but I didn't need to contribute any money to it. The thing would have won with or without me.

A few more battles have yet to be fought to finish the pot-legalization job in the United States. I'm confident that a new generation of activists and financiers can get it done without my help. But there is still more work to be done before our side can claim victory in the drug war. That declaration can't be made until all the prisoners of that war—especially the ones whose primary "offense" was related to marijuana—have been liberated.

— 9 —

The Price of Betrayal

Forty years in, the Men's Wearhouse looked strong as ever. When it came to selling men's clothing, we were the New York Yankees of the 1950s, the Roman Empire on Julius Caesar's return from Gaul, Michael Jackson with the release of *Thriller*. We flat-out dominated.

But as winter turned to spring in 2013, tension wracked the highest levels of the corporation at our dual headquarters (in our traditional base in Houston and in Fremont, California, where I had moved most of our executive command when I relocated to Oakland in the early eighties). Some of the disagreement we laid out on the table, like the one between myself and our senior management team about how much they should be paid. Some of it played out behind my back, like the nutty move to cut me out of our marketing strategy.

A series of health problems and, admittedly, my own diminishing enthusiasm for the CEO job led me to take a step away from the day-to-day operation of the Men's Wearhouse. I stuck around as executive chairman of the board and of course continued to do our TV commercials. I hand-picked a new CEO from within the company. It turned out that the new guy, Doug Ewert, and I had very different ideas about how to lead the Men's Wearhouse into the future.

I thought Doug and I would be able to work through our competing visions for the company. I thought wrong. Ewert buddied up with our lead director, Bill Sechrest, whom I brought into the company as a board member some ten years earlier. It was the two of them, I believe, who orchestrated my ouster.

I've got to say—they were good.

By the time I saw it coming, it was too late.

• • •

It was late on a Monday afternoon in June of 2013. Early evening, really, around 6 PM, and the board of directors of the Men's Wearhouse had called me in ahead of their biannual meeting the next day to tell me that they had come to a resolution about my future.

Speaking for the board, Sechrest told me, "The company has two leaders, you and Doug, and has been pulled in two directions. We want to have one leader, and we are going to go with Doug. We would like you to resign as executive chairman of the board."

Sechrest told me that I could retain the title of chairman emeritus, keep my access to the company jet, and, of course, continue to do the commercials—all on a one-year, $1 million contract. He gave me four hours to make up my mind: take the offer, or you're fired.

I can't say the move came as a total shocker. Two years earlier, I'd appointed Ewert to succeed me as our CEO. I stayed on as executive chairman of the board and retained a strong voice when it came to mapping the future of the company. Tensions had been building between us for more than a year, and at our most recent board meeting in April 2013, it had become very clear that Ewert and I had developed irreconcilable differences when it came to the future of the Men's Wearhouse. Like Abraham Lincoln said, "A house divided against itself cannot stand," and the leadership of the Men's Wearhouse was very clearly divided. The two-headed structure of the company suited me just fine. But it looked to me like Doug went to the board on his own and convinced them that it no longer worked for him.

I called our corporate lawyer at ten o'clock that Monday night before the next day's board meeting, and told him: I would not resign.

My final, fateful meeting as the leader of the Men's Wearhouse took place the next morning at 9 AM in a soulless conference room in what used to be the W Hotel on the edge of the Silicon Valley marshlands. If you're looking for a good place to dump a body, you couldn't do much better than the Newark, California, waterfront. That's where my hand-picked board of directors dumped mine.

When I walked into that conference room, I knew I was a goner. I took my seat at the table and placed my head in the noose. By 9:05, they had pulled the lever on the trapdoor and I was swinging from the gallows. Bill Sechrest stood to his full six-foot-seven height and read from a piece of paper, "The board of directors by unanimous consent has decided to replace you as executive chairman of the board and terminate your employment."

Officiously, he informed me, "Your office furniture and possessions have been placed in storage."

Before I left the room, one of the directors asked if I could stick around first to answer some questions. That struck me as kind of an odd request, but I figured, what the hell, and pulled up a chair and mumbled off a few answers to questions that have slipped my mind in the moment's fog. I got up to leave, and on my way out another board member asked me if there was any chance that I'd ever be able to work with any of those people again.

I looked them all in the eye, one by one:

There was Bill Sechrest, Texas lawyer, Stanford grad, cofounding trustee of the World Business Academy, former board member of the Esalen Institute. He also wrote a couple of metaphysical books that caught my attention. I met him, and I liked him, and I not only put him on our board in 2004, but helped arrange for him to become the board chair at the Institute of Noetic Sciences. We'd known each other for twenty-five years. There once was a time when I felt like he and I were soul mates, especially in our shared belief in the World Business Academy's mission of businesses taking care of the whole of society. Now, here he was, serving as trigger man on the drive-by.

Rinaldo Brutoco, the founder of the World Business Academy, an environmental guy, writer, lecturer, worked out of Santa Barbara. He had been on our board from the time we went public twenty-one years earlier. He started a few businesses and wrote a few books, and he's the one who strongly influenced me into establishing the commission system at the Men's Wearhouse. I once lent him $350,000 to buy a condo in Hawaii and forgave the debt, before he sold it for $2 million. What did Dante say in the *Inferno* about the betrayal of the benefactor?

Shelley Stein, a liquor distributor down in Dallas, was the old underwriter from Bear Stearns who handled our IPO. It's customary to put somebody from the bank on your board, and I had no problem with adding Shelley to ours in 1995. He became the chair of our compensation committee. He thought the senior executive staff of the Men's Wearhouse should be paid more, and I disagreed.

The CEO I chose to replace me, Doug Ewert, was a career merchant who came into the Men's Wearhouse as a tie buyer. He earned his way to the top through hard work. To be honest, he wasn't my first choice for the job. I always saw him as more of a chief operating officer type than a CEO, somebody who was good at keeping a place running as it always had been but who could not envision a strategy for the future. It could have worked out between us, if only Doug could have survived on $2.5 million a year. It was more than four times the salary that I ever made in that job, but he saw it as a pittance. He compared himself to the kings of finance and industry who at that time were riding a high-speed elevator to the top of the wealth and income inequality pyramid. They lived in the penthouse of the top tenth of the top 1 percent, and Doug—in my view—wanted in.

The vice chairman of the board, David Edwab, was the former president and chief financial officer of the Men's Wearhouse and, sad to say, my former best friend in the world. Dave saved our bacon when the banks almost took us under in the early 1980s. He directed our transition from a private to a public company, which led to our supercharged growth.

Then there was Dr. Deepak Chopra, physician, professional wise man, acclaimed writer, and maybe a mystic. I met him through the Institute of Noetic Sciences, and I felt he would lend an ethicist's perspective to our operation at the Men's Wearhouse. I put him on the board the same time as Bill Sechrest, in 2004. Although he wasn't actually present the day of my official termination, he had visited me the night before in my hotel room in Newark, imploring me in a "guided meditation" to consider my legacy in making my decision.

Two other board members were included in that unanimous vote against me, but I harbor no animosity whatsoever against them: Michael Ray, the Stanford professor of creativity who had been with the Men's Wearhouse since our beginning as a public company, and Grace Nichols, the CEO behind the rise of Victoria's Secret, whom we brought on as a director in 2011 to add a much-needed woman's point of view. The two of them, as I understand it, mainly went along for the ride. Ray left the board not long after my departure.

My strongest ally on the board had been Larry Katzen, an accountant from the old school whom we added to the lineup in 2006 to make sure we complied with the Sarbanes-Oxley Act's truth-in-auditing requirements, enacted in wake of the Enron collapse. Sechrest bounced Larry out of there just before me, after Katzen sought to resolve my differences with Doug by proposing that the board actually hear us both out. Last thing those guys wanted was fairness and honesty. Who knows if Larry would have made a difference at the end. Probably not.

Like I said, I looked everybody in the room right in the eye, considering my reply to the question of whether I could work with any of them again. They must have been kidding. Work with them again? I would barely speak to any of them again. And I damn near haven't.

I gave them my one-word answer:

"No."

When I retreated to my room in the hotel, the great quote from Groucho Marx came to mind: "I don't want to belong to any club that would accept me as a member." I kind of twisted it around. I didn't want to belong to any club with people like these as its members—even if I was the one who'd invited them into our gang in the first place.

How did everything lead up to that big "no" in the hotel conference room in Newark in the late spring of 2013?

I've retraced the journey in my mind maybe a hundred thousand times. The road was fairly straight, and it wasn't that winding, but it had plenty of warning signs.

• • •

In our first decade of operation, all of us original principals in the founding and launch of the Men's Wearhouse shared the same sense of urgency to see the operation survive. The same sense of excitement to watch it flourish. The same sense of trust in each other, the pride that we had built something that would last beyond our lifetimes. I felt that our company had evolved into something more than just a money-making operation. Our company had soul. We cared about everybody—our employees, our customers, our communities. We had established an example for the World Business Academy to show how a company could take responsibility for the whole of society as well as the pocketbooks of its investors. Even when we went public, I never felt that we had to sacrifice our belief in a sustainable business practice. Like it said in our mission statement that I scrawled on the back of the cocktail napkin, we wanted to "maximize sales, provide value to our customers, and deliver top quality customer service," while at the same time we wanted to have fun and maintain values such as "nurturing creativity" and "enhancing a sense of community" and "striving toward becoming self-actualized people." My whole career at the Men's Wearhouse, I instigated a corporate culture designed to keep the executive staff in close contact with the needs and wants of the men and women on our front lines, the employees who interfaced with our customers. No matter what, our employees and our customers had to be in the front of our mind in every decision that we made.

Over time, I felt that the driving impulse of our company had begun to change around me, and in ways that I didn't like. I tried to ignore my concerns, stuffing them deep down inside to worry about later.

My unease first became palpable, in my memory, in the latter part of 2006, when I flew out to Houston to visit our new corporate headquarters. I had tasked our chief financial officer, Neill Davis, with finding new offices to accommodate the accounting, human resources, and IT staffs of our growing company. These departments had all been working out of a warehouse that serviced our nearby national distribution center, and it was time to upgrade their working environment.

As soon as I walked into the new building on Rogerdale Road in southwest Houston, I was revolted. I mean I literally wanted to throw up. Talk about overdoing it—Neill's interior designers had gone completely overboard. He must have spent at least $5 million, maybe $10 million, with eleven-foot ceilings and leather furniture and kitchenettes with microwaves sprinkled around the place like fairy dust. And for what? It's not like they were ever going to be bringing anybody into the building to sell them a suit. Or to purchase fabric. Or to do anything that had anything to do with production, sales, distribution, or acquisitions. This kind of thing just didn't happen in our industry. Retail is a low-margin business. Insurance, banking, the law—they run out of gigantic glass offices with crystal and leather, mainly because their higher margins can afford it and *that's where they do their business*. We did ours in our stores.

My whole time at the Men's Wearhouse, we did our offices on the cheap. At the beginning, we ran our corporate headquarters out of a backroom office in our first store, on Westheimer Road. It wasn't much bigger than a walk-in closet in Beverly Hills. Richie and Harry and I did our work in there with a few other folks behind used metal desks that we bought for like $25 each—and we moved them into the store ourselves. Now we were going Taj Mahal? It made me feel like the company was having an identity crisis.

I made my rounds the day of the visit and shook hands and had my picture taken with people in the office, all with a smile on my face. That was my job. But beneath my phony smile, I felt an inconsolable sadness, self-doubt, and a sense that the culture I had shaped over the previous thirty-four years was beginning to crumble.

This new office, in my mind, represented an intentional defiance of what had been the culture of our company. And here was Neill and everybody else busting their buttons while they showed me around the place. How could they possibly think I'd like it? Was I that poor of a communicator? Had I fallen this far out of touch with my own company?

If so, I thought to myself beneath the smile, maybe it was time for me to resign.

• • •

Maybe my problem was physical.

The first decade of the new millennium didn't treat my body so well. I underwent open abdominal surgery four times. And right when I'd recovered from all of those, I ruptured my Achilles tendon running for safety during an earthquake in Hawaii. It put me on the disabled list for several months.

First, an abdominal aortic aneurysm. I'd felt the pulsing in the bottom of my belly when I was on vacation in Hawaii in 2002. Soon as I got home to the Bay Area, I had it checked out, and I had to go under the knife. I recovered pretty nicely, or so I thought, until three years later, when I was at an Oakland A's baseball game and I felt a pain in my leg. I asked a doctor friend of mine, Tom Lewis, to take a look at it, and upon further examination, he found a boil on my left side. It made Tom think that the boil and the leg pain might be related to the graft that had been part of the surgery three years earlier to fix my aneurysm. Turned out Tom was right: my left bifurcation graft was infected, and that infection had gotten into my blood. They rushed me to the hospital and plugged an antibiotic drip into my arm to head off the very high possibility of sepsis. Then, emergency surgery—a femoro-femoral bypass to get my blood flowing right.

Once I recovered from the fem-fem, I flew to the Mayo Clinic for the big fix. Tom and another doctor pal, Ray Logger, who had first diagnosed my abdominal aortic aneurysm, accompanied me on the trip to Rochester, Minnesota, where the clinics team, led by vascular surgeon Dr. Peter Gloviczki, totally replaced my original graft. The thing I'll always remember about the Mayo experience, even more than the hundred-foot

high atrium when you walk in, and the soothing sounds of the piano players everywhere you go in the hospital, was sitting with Ray in a courtyard
with a forest of IV lines running out of my arms and me wanting to down
a Pepsi more than anything in the world. Ray got me one to swish around
in my mouth and spit out like a boxer on his stool between rounds. Sugar
never tasted so sweet.

I'd pretty much recovered from the repair job at the Mayo Clinic when
we discovered another problem: this time an intestinal blockage caused by a
bowel adhesion, related to the abdominal aortic aneurysm surgeries. Compared to the "AAA" fix and then the two grafts, the blockage was small
beans, although it did require them to cut my gut open again. Once the
adhesion cleared, I did such a good job recovering that another one formed,
requiring another open abdominal surgery.

Yes, I was getting tired of getting my belly split up the middle, and I figured I deserved a long rest. Lorri and I split for Hawaii. We were enjoying a
cup of coffee out on the veranda of our beachfront home when, what do you
know—an earthquake. I'm not sure of the magnitude, but it was big enough
to make us run for cover. In our sprint away from the house, my Achilles
popped. After the surgery, a walking boot became the newest fixture in my
wardrobe. I did not like the way I looked, limping around into the next year.

• • •

Sitting around recovering from six major surgeries in five years, you find
that you've got a lot of time to think. Me, I could have modeled for Rodin,
I did so much sitting and thinking. Amid the pondering, I came to a couple
of realizations: I was wearing down physically, and I needed to plan my
succession.

I've heard it said that choosing a replacement is the most important
decision a CEO will ever make. Well, if that's the case, I sure botched mine.

My biggest screwup, I have come to see in retrospect, is that as the
Men's Wearhouse blossomed into greatness, I failed to make sure that my
top-level executives shared my values and beliefs, which I observed in stark
terms during my tour of the new Rogerdale Road headquarters. Even if I
had never consciously articulated a specific stakeholder-capitalistic concept,
we certainly practiced it by my own force of will. But as we grew, it dawned
on me, suddenly, that I was surrounded by a phalanx of suited professional

executives recruited from the ranks of corporate America, and that a lot of these people—maybe even most of them—weren't on board with what we were trying to do from a stakeholder point of view. They ragged me behind my back. Called me crazy. Disdained our programs that distributed income and wealth downward. Thought they were underpaid. Were overly wedded to maximized shareholder value. None of them truly believed in what I believed in, beyond the margins—beyond lip service—in leveraging our business to improve society as a whole.

Remember how you have to believe something before you see it? Well, they didn't believe, and they didn't see. To be sure, they knew how to merchandise, how to govern our financial arrangements, how to improve our technology, how to drive revenue and profits, and how to take care of our shareholders. How to take care of all the items of executive function that go into the operation of a major corporation. That's why I hired them. But seven years after my termination, I'm only beginning to see how, at the end of my forty-year tenure, they had no clue about the coming ascendency of stakeholder capitalism. They didn't share the depth of my feeling for our frontline employees—the wardrobe consultants, the tailors, hard-working folks in the warehouses and distribution centers. I think they lost touch with our customers, the guy who had a job interview that week and needed to look and feel at his best. They didn't *feel* the road man who wanted to show us a lineup of shirts or ties or shoes, or how the prosperity of his kids' future depended on him making that sale. They didn't absorb what it meant for the country when, at last count, 1 percent of the nation's population held 40 percent of its wealth. My bad was that I never confronted any of this dispassion. I allowed it to fester, and in the end, it resulted in my ouster and the destruction of our company.

I compounded my mistake by limiting the search for my replacement to in-house candidates. There was one guy who might have worked out—Eric Lane, our chief operating officer and president. I had hired him out of the Macy's executive training program and started him out as a store manager in Marin County. He didn't much care for the assignment, but I told him that this is the way you earn your respect on your way up. He got that, and came to excel there and at every other stop on his rise almost to the top. We moved him to a regional manager's position in San Diego before we sent him back to Houston for some executive and merchandise training and experience. I really liked Eric—tough guy, football player in high school.

I always thought he could have been the guy. Then he pulled a fast one on me and retired, in 2007, and moved to Boise where he coached his two sons' high school football team. I actually admired the hell out of him for that. Eric knew himself and knew what was the most important thing in his life: his family.

Pre-Eric, I long held another possibility for my CEO replacement in mind. You might remember Charlie Bresler as my partner on the "Teen Tour" of North America when I was thirteen, the bridge-playing pal I shared my first drunk with down in the Bahamas, on that horrible Harveys Bristol Cream. Charlie ended up doing pretty well for himself. He got his PhD in clinical and social psychology and wound up with a therapist's practice in Fresno, when he saw me on TV and gave me a call. I got back in touch with him and recruited him to become our human resources director, our sales managing trainer, and later still, our president, to replace Eric. But people started coming up to me randomly, calling me out of nowhere, and telling me: please don't make Charlie our boss. Unfortunately, it seemed like Charlie wasn't going to work out.

I looked very hard at David Edwab. After all, we did go back thirty years. We were best friends, or so I thought. He grew up in the greater New York area—always a plus, in my view. Dave, of course, led the way for us as our chief financial officer when we went public, and he later served as my number two as chief operating officer. I even gave him the title of president. Dave left us in 2000 to go to work for Bear Stearns as the head of the retail investment banking group, a move that certainly should have been a warning sign about where his heart was at. That whole world of hostile takeovers and leverage and derivative financing is completely inimical to the type of long-term capitalistic sustainability that I tried to foster at the Men's Wearhouse. I was heartened when he said he missed the corporate culture of the Men's Wearhouse after a couple of years at Bear Stearns. I was happy to bring him back as our vice chairman in 2002. When it came time to pick a future CEO, however, I eliminated Dave due to his lack of experience in merchandising—in actually working in the stores. He did not know what "selling with soul" meant. He was a numbers guy who didn't appreciate the importance of culture nearly as much as he did the bottom line.

By default, then, the job would go to Doug Ewert, the old tie buyer, who had put together a terrific resume. In 1995, we snatched him away from

Macy's in San Francisco, where he was a senior men's clothing merchant. We made him a buyer and a planner. We promoted him to general merchandise manager, senior VP of merchandising, executive VP and COO of the K&G brand stores that we had acquired in 1999, executive VP and COO of the entire company, and then president, in place of Charlie, who dropped down to executive vice president.

It would have been about 2008 when I began to settle, in my own mind, on Doug as the guy. I'd been telling him at our training meetings at Chaminade that he had the makings of a future CEO. We clicked, me as the CEO looking out for the future, and him as COO, making sure that we kept doing what we'd always been doing as efficiently as possible. I mean, Doug was a terrific COO. He did a great job managing the day-to-day while I kept the tiller pointed in the right direction. The only question I had was whether he had the magic touch that a CEO needed to set the course for a company.

Sometime early in 2011, I told Doug I was ready to make the move. I'd step down as CEO and turn it over to him, and I later helped negotiate him a new compensation package of around $2.5 million. I'd stick around as executive chairman, to maintain our core values and do the TV commercials. Doug sounded thrilled with the arrangement, and we went to the board for approval.

On June 15, 2011, I handed him the keys to the Men's Wearhouse.

• • •

For the first year, the new arrangement worked out okay between Doug and me, but not without one little flareup that made me begin to realize that picking Doug might have been a blunder.

Back in '95, it was Eric Lane who hired Doug into the company. Eric, after he left the Men's Wearhouse and had been up in Boise a few years, decided his family could use a little extra cash. He asked Doug if maybe he could do some part-time work. I'd have found something for him in a second, if it was my call, but it wasn't. It was Doug's, and Doug was adamant—no way.

I remember talking to Doug about it, and saying, "Doug—Eric hired you."

Doug's response: "So what?"

I had never taken Doug for a "so what" kind of guy.

Around the middle of 2012, my disagreements with Doug went beyond "so what." In fact, they got pretty ugly.

Let's start with an area where things often break down in the business world, and that is money. In Doug's case, he and the executive team whose water he carried—they wanted a lot more of it.

Executive compensation has always been a fairly touchy topic with me. Mine at the end was recorded in the SEC reports as $1.8 million a year. Only $600,000 of that was actual salary. The other two-thirds paid for my insurance and my use of the company airplane. Of course, I could always sell some stock if I wanted or needed more money for anything, but I always held my salary proportional to what our one-thousand-plus store managers made, a ratio of about twelve to one, which created a culture of fairness and trust.

We were far more generous when it came to Doug, presenting him in 2011 with a total reported compensation package of $5,355,481 that was mostly made up of a substantial one-time stock award of more than $3.6 million. The next year, with far less generous stock components, his reported compensation came down to about $2.1 million, which was more than I ever made, but apparently not enough for Doug's survival. He came to me at the end of 2012 and asked for a new package of $4.5 million. There was no way I'd recommend him to the board for that much, and I told him so. He doesn't think our rank-and-file workers check out the public filings on how much we make?

Our dispute over his pay was just the beginning of our difficulties. He wanted to sell off our K&G stores. I thought it was a bad idea. K&G, an even lower-cost brand than the Men's Wearhouse, served a unique community and protected us from potential competitors at the lower end of the suit-buying spectrum. Then Doug wanted to cut back on our annual "Aloha Award" of Hawaiian vacations, from two hundred to one hundred employees, and I thought that was nuts—the awards were a huge hit at our holiday parties and a huge morale booster. Not to be outdone by himself, Doug, without even asking me, brought in an outside consultant to discuss a refashioning of our marketing campaigns. You'd think they might want to bring the face of the company into these conversations.

As the calendar ran out on 2012, the tension had grown fairly thick between us, which made for an unhealthy work environment at our (more austere) executive offices in Fremont. We met individually with the board of directors and came to a rapprochement, but it only lasted a few months. Our cold war was about to erupt into flames.

• • •

I might have picked all these people for the board, but I guess you never know what you're going to get when you gather a bunch of geniuses into a room and pay them all $200,000 plus a year to guide you on how to run your company, even though some of them don't know the first thing about business. (Hello, Deepak.)

Shelley Stein, what else could you say about a Bear Stearns alumnus other than that he had the heart of an investment banker? Dave Edwab, so much for a "best friend" who I thought would protect me from the coup. I think Rinaldo Brutoco had a good heart, but he checked it at the door when the deal went down on me. The diabolical Bill Sechrest, my brother in noetic sciences—I guess for him science and spirit met at the intersection of greed and self-dealing.

But the way I heard it, my ouster was primarily a Ewert-Sechrest production, motivated by the deadly sin of greed.

Doug never got over my opposition to his pay demand. He found an ally in his campaign to increase his own pay in our lead director, Sechrest, who himself was dissatisfied with the $212,000 compensation he received every year for his fairly minimal board member duties.

By early 2013, the two of them were apparently meeting once a week. I'm told Doug laid it on thick with Bill about all the things I wouldn't let him do. According to Doug, I didn't respect upper management, and upper management was pissed at me. I got my money when the Men's Wearhouse went public, the story went, and now I wouldn't let anyone else get theirs.

Aligned with each other, Doug and Bill brought Edwab and Stein into their circle, their displeasure with me stoked even further by other aspects of my public life.

For one thing, I remained a notorious pothead, and I contributed another $50,000 to the failed recreational marijuana legalization ballot measure in 2010. On top of my advocacy of the herb, I'd also publicly taken up the cause for the therapeutic use of MDMA, the hallucinogenic widely known as ecstasy with which I had experimented (and very much liked).

For another—and this really would have gotten under the skin of the kingpins of investment—I supported the Occupy Wall Street movement in the fall of 2011. I'd met with and advised some of the leaders, and provided material support to the occupiers' encampment at Zuccotti Park. When the movement spread across the country the next year, we posted a "We Stand with Occupy Wall Street" sign in the window of our downtown Oakland store during a raucous demonstration (which didn't keep it from getting shattered by the black-maskers in the bunch).

I think it also concerned Doug and Bill and the rest that by the spring of 2013, I had begun to more fully understand and articulate what stakeholder capitalism was all about. For years I'd been saying that any decision we made had to benefit at least three of our stakeholder groups. The executive types would humor me to my face, but word got back to me that once I left the room, they'd dismiss it behind my back.

Confronted with the increasingly shareholder-focused mindset and self-interested thinking of the Men's Wearhouse's leadership, I knew there was no way there would be any positive restructuring with this crew. If I truly wanted to rebuild the company into a model of stakeholder capitalism, I realized I'd have to try and take the Men's Wearhouse private, an increasingly popular idea in corporate America thanks to the rising volume of private equity cash.

I looked around for some investment experts to give me an assessment. I'd always thought that we were seriously undervalued at $1.4 billion, and damn if they didn't agree with me. They told me that we could get a 30 to 40 percent premium on our stock price, which was selling for about $30 a share at the time. This would have amounted to about a billion-dollar increase in our valuation, and a windfall for our shareholders, if you want to look at it from their perspective.

I called the board members on a satellite phone from the corporate jet on a flight to New York—which turned out to be one of the dumbest things I've ever done in my life. Instead of them being excited about the deal like I thought they would be, they freaked out. They concluded that I'd get rid of them all once I regained control of the company.

The showdown was set—it was either them or me.

• • •

I had a pretty good idea going into our April 2013 board meeting—the last one before my firing—that I was on thin ice. By the time the session concluded, it had started to crack.

Compensation Committee chair Shelley Stein kicked off his presentation with a recitation of the proposed new bonus-laden packages for the executive staff. The board eventually signed off on what turned out to be a 73 percent increase in Doug's total pay to $3.6 million. It more than tripled board vice chairman Edwab's total to $1.9 million. Sechrest, as lead director, would receive a 25 percent increase, to $336,857. Stein, as compensation chairman, teed himself up for a 28 percent raise, to $272,155.

In an apparent attempt to buy me off, Shelley recommended a $1 million raise for the executive board chairman.

The revelation surprised, insulted, and disgusted me. Bill tried to blow past the compensation part of the program to the rest of the agenda, but I interjected. First, I asked for a more detailed breakdown on the different components that went into the compensation figures—salary, bonuses, stock incentives, and the like. As our company attorney, Michael Conlon, graciously sought to provide them, I wondered aloud whether the executives' bonuses had been factored into the performance targets we had just provided to Wall Street analysts, given that we normally lowballed our earnings estimates by 5 percent to account for the company-wide bonuses that would appropriately be approved later in the year. In this instance—and contrary to our past practices—it appeared to me as if the bonuses *had* been worked into the projection we gave to Wall Street. The shifty implication was pretty clear: we would have to substantially cut back on the bonuses to our frontline employees this year in order to pay for the outrageous increases that we were shoveling to the executives.

My question hung in the air. It fell to our acting CFO, Diane Wilson, to answer.

"That's right, George," Diane snapped. Her tone was indignant. "We used the same performance targets for both Wall Street and the senior execs. I've been doing the bonus computation for fifteen years, and we've only hit the 'excellent' bonus once."

It was a deceptive answer, designed to obfuscate the reality of what was going on: an upward distribution of the company's wealth at the expense of the most valuable employees in our company, the 85 percent of the people who actually did the work, who distributed and sold the clothes and managed the stores—and who annually received bonuses, even if not in the "excellent" category. Not only was she deceitful, but her disdainful tone signaled that she had been directed to put me in my place if I did any squawking.

I'd heard enough.

If I knew anything, it was that I did not want to be part of what they were doing, and I needed to let them know that I wouldn't be a part of it.

"I thought you knew me better," I concluded, "than to think I could be bribed for a million dollars."

As the words fluttered off my tongue, I could see that I had talked myself into the end of my career at the Men's Wearhouse.

• • •

A couple of weeks before the June board meeting, I got a phone call from Shelley Stein. He told me that "for the time being," the board's plan was that I'd hang on as the executive board chairman at about my same pay. I also learned of a letter that Bill Sechrest had distributed to the other board members. It basically said that they needed to make a strong show of support for Doug, to communicate to him and the rest of the world that he was their guy, that all the power of the company was being transferred to him—including all advertising decisions—and that I would not be allowed to set foot in the executive offices in Fremont. They would give me an office in downtown San Francisco, with a secretary, but I would no longer have any say over company operations. Also, I couldn't talk to anybody on the executive team anymore without first cleaning it with Sechrest.

Then came that Monday in June 2013 meeting, when Sechrest told me the two-headed company wasn't working and they'd have to chop one of them off—mine. He presented me with the chairman emeritus offer and the pitch-man proviso, with the 10 PM deadline to make up my mind, to accommodate a rescheduling of the stockholders meeting that had been set for Wednesday, to scratch my name from the ballot.

It would only be a one-year deal, the terms of which required me to play like I was okay with Doug. I knew there was no way I'd resign, but I asked for some time to think it over, and they gave me the four hours.

Back in my hotel room, I called my wife to tell her that it was happening.

Over the next four hours, I had a couple other very interesting conversations.

Deepak Chopra called and asked if he could come up to my room. Sure, I told him, and not long afterward, he was in my hotel suite, running me through the "guided meditation." He had me sit in a chair with my back straight and my eyes closed and my feet flat on the floor. As my body relaxed and my mind cleared, Deepak focused my attention on my legacy at the Men's Wearhouse. It was then, with the clarity of mind that Deepak helped foster, that I came to the realization that Doug Ewert had been a great chief operations officer, but that he didn't have the vision, the courage, or the charisma to make it as a CEO.

Twenty minutes into the meditation, Deepak told me I could open my eyes, and he asked if I'd like to share with him any of my realizations.

"I realized," I said, "that Doug cannot be the CEO of the Men's Wearhouse. I think I made a mistake when I recommended him."

I don't think it was the realization that Deepak was hoping for. He responded that the issue of Doug's position had already been decided, and that what I needed to be concerned about at that moment was my legacy and what I needed to do to protect it. I interpreted that to mean that Deepak thought I should take the offer and entrust my legacy to Doug's care.

I almost trembled in terror.

If this was my legacy we were talking about, I thought that mine would be left in tatters by the direction Ewert and Sechrest were taking with the Men's Wearhouse, down the path of greed. The way I saw it, they would destroy the Men's Wearhouse, at least in the form that I had known and loved. The generations of workers and customers and suppliers who knew it from its heyday, they'd all get old and die, and the ensuing generations would never know it existed except for whatever account winds up on Wikipedia.

If this was about my legacy, as Deepak suggested, if it was about the life and spirit of George Zimmer, it was almost like I had no choice but to allow for my expungement to occur at their hands, so that I could preserve the true version of who I was and what I did.

I told Deepak flat out: "I won't work for Doug."

I don't specifically remember the details of Deepak's departure from my hotel room, only that it was the last time we ever spoke. He did send me a card a year or two later, inviting me to resume our relationship. I ignored it.

No sooner had Deepak closed the door behind him than Rinaldo Brutoco called with pretty much the same pitch: the board had made its decision, and it was up to me to "protect" myself and my legacy. I told him I didn't need any protection. I also told him I couldn't work for Doug.

When the clock struck ten that night, I called Mike Conlon, the lawyer. I told him I wouldn't resign, and that I'd see them at my firing in the morning.

• • •

The Men's Wearhouse's annual shareholders meetings had been scheduled for Wednesday, June 19, but that obviously wasn't going to happen, not with the executive chairman of the board having been fired and no longer a candidate for a directorship. Being a public company, the board had to put out a statement about the cancellation. It included some news:

"The Board of Directors of Men's Wearhouse (NYSE:MW) today announced that it has terminated George Zimmer from his position as executive chairman," they said in the first paragraph of the three-paragraph release. "The Board expects to discuss with Mr. Zimmer the extent, if any, and terms of his ongoing relationship with the Company."

So, I was officially out. The release went on to say that the shareholders meeting had been postponed "to re-nominate the existing slate of directors without Mr. Zimmer."

Once the press release went out, I countered with a one-paragraph statement of my own:

> Over the last 40 years, I have built the Men's Wearhouse into a multi-billion-dollar company with amazing employees and loyal customers who value the products and service they receive at the Men's Wearhouse. Over the past several months I have expressed my concerns to the Board about the direction the company is currently heading. Instead of fostering the kind of dialogue in the Boardroom that has, in part, contributed to our success, the Board has inappropriately chosen to silence my concerns by terminating me as an executive officer.

The story went worldwide, and I got calls of support from all over the globe. Befuddlement colored the first-day coverage, with nobody understanding why this comfortable presence that had been welcomed into America's living rooms had been extinguished without explanation. Thousands of employees, customers, and just plain folk who liked the way I looked on TV bombarded the internet with expressions of outrage. Late-night TV comic Jimmy Kimmel told his viewers, "It was like firing Santa Claus." I likened it more to Kellogg's axing Tony the Tiger.

I guess the blowback shook up the junta. They came back with a second press release six days later.

In their "further comments regarding the termination of George Zimmer," the directors said they never intended "to hurt George Zimmer." Then, some blah, blah, blah about the "best interests" of the company, before they launched into me.

"Mr. Zimmer," they said, "had difficulty accepting the fact that Men's Wearhouse is a public company with an independent Board of Directors and that he has not been the Chief Executive Officer for two years. He advocated for significant changes that would enable him to regain control, but ultimately he was unable to convince any of the Board members or senior executives that his positions were in the best interests of employees, shareholders or the company's future."

I don't want to get all defensive about it, and it is true that in the end I did want to take the Men's Wearhouse private again. But I do have to take issue with them on a few points.

For one, I don't see how they can say I had difficulty accepting the company's public status when I was the one who took it public in the first place. And as for me accepting the board's independence, I guess I did have a problem with it when the directors veered off the course that we had been charting together for more than twenty years. The CEO job? I'd planned my departure from the position for more than a decade before I stepped down in 2011, and I certainly didn't want to return to being the hands-on boss.

I also found it curious that in their eyes, I was the one who "advocated for significant changes." The only "significant changes" that came between us were the ones that *they* proposed and I opposed—the increase in executive pay, and the decision to sell K&G.

They said I didn't support Doug and the "key management team." I guess that could be seen as a matter of opinion. Sure, I disagreed with them on occasion, and argued my case when issues came up. But once a decision was made, I went along with it.

They said I "expected veto power over significant corporate decisions." Not only did I not have any such expectation, but I had no legal authority to exercise it.

They said they made "considerable efforts" to allow me "to continue to have a significant involvement" with the company. That's true (even if they wanted to exile me to a distant office in San Francisco), but the emeritus deal was only a one-year offer.

"As we stated," the press release concluded, "we fully support Doug Ewert, our CEO, and senior management team who are unified and focused on the future of the company and the best interest of our shareholders, employees and customers."

Like I told Deepak after my guided meditation, I do think I made a mistake in picking Doug to succeed me, and I also think history proved that Doug was the wrong guy to provide for the future of the Men's Wearhouse. When he finally got his chance to set the course for the company, he ran it off a cliff.

I'll leave it up to the public, our employees, and everyone else to determine whether those decisions would have been "in the best interests" of "the company's future." When I got fired, the Men's Wearhouse was worth $2.5 billion. The last time I checked, the value of the bankrupt company had deteriorated to almost nothing.

• • •

Jos. A. Bank Clothiers, Inc., had been around for more than sixty-five years by the time we birthed the Men's Wearhouse in 1973. It had about sixteen stores then, mostly of the factory-outlet variety, including one in my adopted hometown of Houston. We'd always been aware of them. They nipped at our ankles a little bit, but we didn't fear them much after we surpassed them in our growth based on our superior quality and value. To be honest, however, we couldn't say we actually beat them on price. Unlike Joe Bank, we weren't into giving you three free suits if you bought one. You may remember the *Saturday Night Live* spoof on how Joe Bank sold its suits so cheaply that you could use them to wipe up household spills and save money on paper towels. Brutal, but funny.

By the time I was fired, they had a little more than half as many stores as we did—628 to be exact, compared to our 1,143—and only sold a billion dollars a year worth of merchandise, which was not even 40 percent of our total. They were profitable, however, and back when we were about the same size, I thought that buying them out was worth a look. We did an examination, and I put it out that if we could get them for $50 million, it would be worth our while. When they asked $75 million, I said forget it. We had similar locations, similar merchandise, similar customers. Rather than buy them at an expense that did not justify the incremental increase in gross profits, I figured we'd be better off just to beat them on the battlefield. Every other time the subject of a Jos. A. Bank takeover came up, I put it to rest.

Toward my end at the Men's Wearhouse, the question about buying Joe Bank came up again. This time, I wanted to gather some hard data on why it was a bad idea. I always felt in my gut that the two of us were going after the same customer, whom we would win over with our once-a-year sale—truly "only once a year," as I pointed out in the *Star Wars*–style TV commercial. I thought it would be dumb for us to buy them out. To prove my contention, I had our video crew go out to a Joe Bank store in San Francisco and interview their customers who had just made a purchase. Sure enough, 85 percent of the respondents said that they also shopped the Men's Wearhouse and that they usually made their game-day decision based on who had what kind of a sale.

The subject of a takeover never came up as a point of disagreement between Doug and me once I made him the CEO. But it sure did three months after he and Bill Sechrest got rid of me, when Joe Bank CEO Bob Wildrick made an unsolicited, $2.3 billion tender for the Men's Wearhouse. Curiously, the amount equated to the same upper-end, 40 percent premium on our stock price that the investment bankers figured our stock was really worth when I talked to them about taking the company private. Doug turned Wildrick down, but a month later, Doug flipped the script and offered Joe Bank around a billion and a half to buy *them* out—what they call the "Pac-Man defense" in the corporate-raider world, to ward off a takeover. Joe Bank played hard to get, at first, before Doug—who, along with other senior executives and their hired guns from the outside, was playing with house money—upped the offer to $1.8 billion. I'd say they overvalued the company, based on Jos. A. Bank's net sales in 2013 of a little over a billion. Not surprisingly, Jos. A. Bank accepted the offer.

Stock in the Men's Wearhouse kicked around at $35 a share for the few months after they fired me, and it shot up to $45 when word got out about the bidding war between the two companies. Doug and his crew hyped the hell out of the deal for the first year or so after the acquisition, and I guess the analysts on Wall Street bought it. With the analysts leading the cheers, the June 2015 stock price on the newly formed parent corporation for the two retailers, Tailored Brands, Inc., soared to a high of just past $64.

Impressed with Doug's handling of the takeover, the Men's Wearhouse board bumped his compensation up to $9.7 million in 2014, including $4.2 million in what the company called "equity" bonuses for pulling off the Jos. A. Bank deal, according to a proxy statement. Bill Sechrest, as chairman of the board, saw his total compensation package rise to $463,000 thanks to the acquisition.

Unfortunately for everybody concerned, the truth about the deal emerged the next year when Jos. A. Bank's sales plummeted.

• • •

If you want a blow-by-blow account on how an overly hyped transaction dissolved into disaster, check out the federal securities fraud lawsuit in the Southern District of Texas, filed by Peter Makhlouf, individually and on behalf of all others similarly situated, against Tailored Brands, Inc., Douglas S. Ewert, and two other Tailored Brands executives, chief financial officer Jon W. Kimmins and chief merchandising officer Mary Beth Blake.

Makhlouf is a Southern California real estate broker who took a beating on his stock in the Men's Wearhouse as a result of the deal. He was joined in the class action by a coplaintiff, the Strathclyde Pension Fund out of Scotland. They charged that Tailored Brands and the three executives repeatedly made "false and misleading statements" once the acquisition was completed that "concealed from investors known trends and uncertainties associated with dramatic shifts in the Jos. A. Bank business model." Makhlouf also charged that the Tailored Brands leadership knew or recklessly disregarded the fact that the acquisition "would necessarily alienate Jos. A. Bank's existing customers and cause catastrophic sales declines of 30% at Jos. A. Bank."

According to the suit, the defendants promised efficiencies that they never delivered. They got rid of Jos. A. Bank's suppliers. They brought in "slim fits" and brand names that Jos. A. Bank customers didn't like. Perhaps most significantly, they eliminated the "buy one, get three free" promotion that was a source of both ridicule and success for Jos. A. Bank.

In the year and a half after the acquisition was completed in June 2014, the Men's Wearhouse had lost $1.5 billion in market capitalization, the suit said.

The bad news of the Men's Wearhouse third-quarter earnings report in 2015 hit like a tsunami. Company-wide sales slipped 20–25 percent, while the earnings-per-share projection missed by 40 percent, all of it mainly due to the decision to lose the "buy one, get three free" promotion at Jos. A. Bank.

The press hammered the company on the news.

As quoted in the complaint, *Dow Jones* reported, "Turns out shoppers are unwilling to visit or buy Jos. A. Bank's shirts and suits unless they were getting lots of free stuff in return," with a blistering follow-up the next day that said, "There's a 40% Off Sale at Men's Wearhouse (MW) today. Unfortunately, it's the retailer's stock."

Following a Men's Wearhouse conference call a month later, a Tigress Financial Partners research highlight said the takeover of Jos. A. Bank "has been an unbelievable example of corporate greed and arrogance by B level players as over $2 billion in equity market value has been destroyed," according to the Makhlouf complaint. The lawsuit also recounted a *Fortune* headline, "Buying Jos. A. Bank Has Been A Catastrophe for Men's Wearhouse," and another from Bloomberg, "Men's Wearhouse Confronts a New Label: 'Uninvestable.'" *Barron's* Trader Extra column called the Men's Wearhouse purchase of Jos. A. Bank "one of the worst mergers of the millennium."

As for myself, I found it all very interesting. I read an analysis that I'm sure was erroneous that there was only a 7 percent customer overlap between the two brands. Remember, when I was the CEO, we produced that video showing that an extremely high percentage of Jos. A. Bank customers also shopped at the Men's Wearhouse. Charitably speaking, I'd say the new research was inadequate, at best. If the research of our video team played out across the national landscape of the Jos. A. Bank empire, it would have made absolutely no sense for anybody to buy several hundred stores that would be competing for the same customer. On the other hand, if there was such little overlap, it would be insane to change the promotional strategy like Tailored Brands did, despite the fun *Saturday Night Live* was having with it. Which I guess is what the plaintiffs' lawyers argued in the securities fraud lawsuit. And if you *did* change the approach, you'd be destroying the brand. That's why I never wanted to buy Jos. A. Bank.

Tailored Brands caught a break, however, when US District Judge Melinda Harmon dismissed the case on the technical ground that the

lawyers for the plaintiffs did not adequately plead that the defendants
intended to deceive the stock-buying public after the takeover deal closed
in June 2014. The judge wrote in her decision that while motive was not a
"dispositive" issue in the case, she could see how Ewert and the two others
acted out of a desire to keep the company healthy long-term. She pref-
aced that statement, however, by writing, "The pressure to perform faced
by defendants, as well as their compensation scheme, may have provided a
motive for them to promote artificially inflated stock prices."

Judge Harmon invited the plaintiffs to amend their complaint. I think
it was lucky for Doug and the gang that they didn't. In June 2018, final judgment was entered and the case was terminated. Three months later, Doug
Ewert announced his resignation as CEO of Tailored Brands.

By then, the stock price had dropped to $25, from the $35.79 when the
board of directors decided they didn't need any more of my advice, on its
way to $3.26 as of Feb. 26, 2020, the first reported date of community spread
of the coronavirus in the United States.

The pandemic, of course, obliterated brick-and-mortar retail from the
mountains to the oceans white with foam. The Men's Wearhouse, however,
had already dropped into its own death spiral. When they fired me, the
company had zero long-term debt. When Doug retired, it was $1.2 billion.

It devastates me that the many thousands of employees of the Men's
Wearhouse who counted on their ESOPs to provide them with a comfortable retirement are now facing their golden years in fear. But don't worry
about Doug. He walked away with a $7.6 million separation package. In
the five years it took him to destroy the company, he made a reported $37.9
million.

That's what I would call the price of betrayal.

—| 10 |—

Generation Next

A bunch of us sat around in our bathing suits and beach chairs, digging our feet into the sands of Mauna Kea on New Year's Day, 2014. As our wives and kids and friends relaxed in the beauty of our surroundings in front of the Big Island resort, I chatted up one member of the entourage about a new business opportunity that I had been pursuing.

Since my firing from the Men's Wearhouse, I'd come across what I thought was the terrific idea of taking the tuxedo rental business online. The old model compelled the customer to make three trips to the store—one to choose a style and get sized up for it, another to go pick up the tux, and a third to return it. For people who hate to go clothes shopping in the first place, it was torture. On the beach, I told my audience of one that you could do the whole thing by punching it up on an app on your cell phone. The idea caught the attention of my fellow beachcomber: Marc Benioff, the founder, chairman, and CEO of Salesforce, the world leader in no-fuss, no-muss cloud computing.

I'd known Marc for several years, as a friend and client, from when I ran the Men's Wearhouse. He'd commiserated with me over the previous months as I sought to recover from the shock of my firing and regain a sense of equilibrium. I had been in a pretty horrible place in the first days and weeks and even months after my firing. I wallowed in self-pity. I thirsted for revenge. I suffered from betrayal. I burned with anger. I sat by my firepit late at night at my home in Piedmont and envisioned my old "friends" such as Dave Edwab and Doug Ewert and Bill Sechrest and Rinaldo Brutoco swimming in the flames of Dante's ninth circle of hell, reserved for them for their betrayal of their benefactor. Believe me, your thinking can get pretty dark when you're cut loose and untethered from the company you created and managed for forty years.

Marc did as much as anybody to try to pull me out of it. His advice had mainly been for me to chill, to recognize that I'd already made my mark in the entrepreneurial world, and that I had earned the right to do nothing other than enjoy the rest of my days. Kick back, relax, absorb your success, he said: the testimonial of ten thousand employees expressing their support for me on Facebook and Instagram and other internet portals was all that a man needed to cement his legacy. Take a bow, Marc suggested, and walk off the stage.

His advice made a lot of sense, and by the dawning of the New Year, I had pulled back from the worst of myself. I'd turned sixty-five, and I could see how maybe Marc was right. Maybe I should forget about the Men's Wearhouse. Maybe I should spike the ball and declare victory.

But as I'm sure Marc could tell by the excitement that brimmed out of me on the beach, I wasn't ready for the rocking chair. The best way for me to ease the pain of my termination from the company I built and the people I loved who had made it work . . . was to do it again!

I told him about my contact with two young entrepreneurs down in Los Angeles who had launched an online tuxedo startup, and how I was thinking about jumping into it as a late-in-life second act to my business career. I explained how the business would work: the customer orders by phone or online, you size them up with an algorithmic app, you send them a tailor's tape to make sure we got the fit right, and if that didn't quite get it, you'd send them the whole damn tailor, right to their door.

As I dove deeper into the detail, I saw a Cheshire-cat grin envelop Marc's fairly sizable face.

"George," he said, "that is a killer idea."

Next thing I knew, Marc had invested $1.5 million into the company that came to be called Generation Tux.

• • •

It would have been an easy thing to do, doing nothing. But my whole life, I'd never been into taking it easy. I put myself on the line in the sixties, in the antiwar protests at Washington University and in Washington, DC. I knocked on doors in unfriendly territory for George McGovern. I started up my own business when I could have enjoyed the comforts of a much easier life working for my father. I could have accepted bad business practices as the way of the world.

When I got fired from the Men's Wearhouse, I could have talked my way onto some board of directors, or do some kind of lecturing gig, or jumped into a million other soft landings that are usually the last call for people in my condition.

None of those ideas appealed to me.

I didn't want to waste away as a director on some board of a company that I didn't know or create. I very much liked to talk to students as I'd been doing regularly at Stanford and Cal. But I was no teacher.

I had to get back into the action.

As a businessman, and even as an unemployed CEO/executive board chairman, your mind gravitates toward opportunity. You're always running numbers in your head or scratching out ideas on notebook paper. You see a problem, your mind bounces toward a solution. You're enthralled by markets. You try to account for their shortcomings. If you're a former member of the World Business Academy, you still envision manners in which your enterprise can provide for society as a whole. You look for ways to create long-term value.

In the initial weeks and months after Newark, I directed a great deal of my mental business energy toward the Men's Wearhouse, and it wasn't positive. Move on? Maybe I wasn't ready yet.

Private equity firms came knocking on my door almost from the day of the ambush. They had read the news stories about my firing. Knowing that one of the big issues between me and my executioners was my plan to take the company private, these guys drooled over the possibilities. We talked. Then along came Bob Wildrick, the CEO from Jos. A. Bank, and his $2.3 billion offer to buy the Men's Wearhouse. Wildrick went public with his play, which triggered the disastrously successful counteroffer from Doug Ewert that resulted in the reverse takeover of Jos. A. Bank by the Men's Wearhouse and drove up the price.

Ousted from my own company, I had to watch from the sidelines while Wildrick and Ewert did battle. Me, I decided to attack from beneath. Since my dismissal, the Men's Wearhouse executive team—no longer encumbered by the yaps of the former executive chairman—had put the company's K&G stores up for sale. It was the move, of course, that I had tried to head off. I thought that brand had a ton of potential. K&G was like the Walmart of men's clothing, its stores supersized at 23,700 square feet each, a good four times bigger than the typical Men's Wearhouse. The way I looked at it in 2013, K&G was kind of like the twenty-first-century version of the Men's Wearhouse: a discount operation that played to all markets, all demographics, with sales prices seventy percent below what you'd pay in a department store. They even undercut the Men's Wearhouse, which by the 1990s had become kind of a regular men's specialty store. I felt I could really do something with that brand if I put all my attention into it.

Tailored Brands asked $90 million for the ninety-seven K&G locations that had done $366 million in sales in 2012. It looked fair enough to me, so I made my play. Knowing that Doug's team would shiver at the sight of me returning from the grave to buy K&G, I enlisted some private equity players from down in Los Angeles to run the deal. It looked like the thing was going to happen, until a few days before it was supposed to close, when Ewert's team found out that I'd hired a beard. Not surprisingly, they turned us down, even though we were willing to pay their price.

Ostensibly, the deal-breaker for them was our refusal to agree to refrain from hiring any Men's Wearhouse employees for four years. Two years, we could have accepted. They insisted on four, which struck me as unreasonable, especially from the perspective of the employees. I'm sure we would have retained most if not all of the K&G employees, who I believe would have been very excited to go to work for me again. I think what worried the Men's Wearhouse is that I would also make a run at some of their non-K&G people and pick off some of their top sellers. I can't say they were wrong, and no doubt, they would have flocked over to K&G in numbers that would have darkened the sky.

Maybe this tells you something about the business sense of the new leadership team at the Men's Wearhouse. First, they wanted to sell the K&G division. Then, they got rid of the pain-in-the-ass founder and executive chairman who insisted on keeping it. Once they pushed me out, they put K&G up for sale. Somebody offered to buy it at their price, and—they nixed the sale.

I guess they looked at it as personal, not strictly business, contrary to Michael Corleone's approach in *The Godfather*. To be perfectly honest about it, I guess I did, too.

. . .

I thought about ice cream sandwiches in the Sunbelt. I considered going into eyeglasses, or at least investing in a chain that sold them. Speaking of glasses, I lamented the shortsightedness of my overseers at the Men's

Wearhouse from back in the day when I'd tried to talk them into buying Peet's, the Northern California–based coffee concern, the second biggest of its kind in the country after Starbucks. We could have had them in 1999 for $300 million. The board thought I was nuts for even bringing it up.

"That George," I could almost hear them say. "He must be stoned again."

Well, yes, I'm sure I was, and maybe they should have had some of what I was smoking. Peet's has turned over twice since then, most recently in 2012 for $1 billion.

About the time I was getting fired at the Men's Wearhouse, those L.A. kids had just started up what I think was the first online tuxedo rental company in the world. They called it the Black Tux, and Marc Benioff was right: it was a killer idea. The Men's Wearhouse had been in the tuxedo rental business for nearly twenty years, and it had really perked up. The year before my termination, we grossed $412 million in tuxedo rentals, with an 80-percent margin—the damn things were making up nearly half the company's profits. I thought my knowledge of the garment business would match up nicely with the technical expertise of the Black Tux boys. I got in touch with them and offered to invest in a very big way. They said they'd be happy to give me 2.5 percent of the company for $250,000. I told them that wasn't even close to what I had in mind. I wanted control of the company.

They did not want to relinquish it. We parted as friends and went our separate ways.

My conversation with Marc Benioff on the beach told me that this online tuxedo idea had some legs to it. His reaction really amped me up. Throughout 2014, I put together a partnership for the rollout of Generation Tux. I threw in a good chunk of my own change—$6 million, to be exact. Plus, Marc Benioff's piece. Plus, I put the arm on a few other friends and associates.

We were ready for takeoff.

. . .

By now, I'd finished reading my friend John Mackey's book *Conscious Capitalism*. It was just the kind of inspiration that I needed, and it rolled off the presses right when I was launching a brand-new business. The timing was perfect. Now I had conscious articulation of what I unconsciously had been doing at the Men's Wearhouse for forty years, and I had the intellectual foundation for what stakeholder capitalism looked like. I already knew what it *felt* like. I saw the construction of Generation Tux as its next testament.

We incorporated the company in the spring of 2014 and established our headquarters, distribution center, and IT offices in Louisville, Kentucky—conveniently located in the middle of the continent. We kept the executive team in downtown Oakland, in an office we put together in the gorgeous old I. Magnin building, an art deco delight.

In early 2015, we forged what we thought would be a game-changing partnership that would get Generation Tux going with a bang. January snow covered the ground when we went to New York for a meeting with Macy's CEO Terry Lundgren, in his office which had been professionally and modestly appointed, unlike that monstrosity of a Men's Wearhouse HQ on Rogerdale Road in Houston. The subject of our meeting: a contract between Generation Tux and Macy's, in which we would rent tuxedos in their stores.

The deal was this: we'd erect kiosks in the suits department of a specified number of Macy's stores that would enable the tux-wearing public to size themselves up and do all their rental paperwork right then and there with the Macy's employees, who would then turn matters over to us to make the delivery. At first, Terry thought we would maintain inventory on their premises, which kind of defeated the purpose of the whole thing. I told him, we don't do frontline inventory. We kept it all back at the distribution center in Louisville.

It looked to me like the lightbulb went on in his head. Nobody, especially him, would have to worry about clogging up the back of the house with racks of tuxedos.

He seemed pleased.

We shook hands on it.

"You're my Silicon Valley boys," Terry told me and my team, smiling.

That we were—for a month, anyway.

I don't know what happened, but thirty days is all it took for Terry to inform us that our deal was off.

No surprise to me, it turned out that the Men's Wearhouse was to blame.

Remember, Doug Ewert was a Macy's alum. So was Mary Beth Blake, the Men's Wearhouse chief merchandising officer. I think some of their old contacts at Macy's ran an end around on Terry to tell Doug and Mary Beth about what was going on between me and their old boss. Admittedly, that's just speculation on my part. But somehow or other, the deal got scotched. Who knows how it happened? All I know for sure is that it did happen, and in June of 2015, Macy's announced it had sealed a tuxedo-rental deal with the Men's Wearhouse, in an arrangement that mirrored the same one I had fashioned.

What's weird is that at the time they got together, the Men's Wearhouse was still the world champion of tuxedo rentals. Can anybody please tell me how a deal with Macy's would make sense for them, other than cutting me off at the knees? The Men's Wearhouse owned the brick-and-mortar tuxedo rental market at the time. Why in the world would they want to share that with Macy's, except to keep Generation Tux out of the game?

Predictably, the deal was a disaster. The Men's Wearhouse had virtually no online presence and no up-and-ready way to ship the suits to the customer. Over the next eighteen months, the arrangement ended up costing Tailored Brands $14 million, while Wall Street analysts attacked the company's stock price as severely inflated.

I had a conversation with Terry after our deal fell through. I had to ask him, what gives? Terry casually explained that it was just business, not personal. He told me that when he and I were talking, back before the Men's Wearhouse muscled in on me, he had to cover all his bases. Sure, he had spoken with us—even made the handshake deal—but he made sure to keep a "no-shop" clause out of the discussion. Nothing prevented him, then, from talking to the Men's Wearhouse, or anybody anywhere else, at the same time he was talking to us. I chalked it up as another lesson learned, a tutorial on the ethical shortcomings of shareholder capitalism.

· · ·

We wanted to launch Generation Tux in September 2014, but a $4 million complication with our computer software system forced us to hold off. There was a mosaic quality that we went for in our website that added to its complexity. Check it out now and you'll know what I mean—it's almost like we are letting the customer be the designer. It can get really wild, especially when you've got brides designing the most important day of their lives. They get to play around with different styles, different fits, different matches, different colors, different articles of clothing, different prices, with or without vests, cummerbunds (pleated or not), and more. You don't want that pocket there? Put it on the other breast—no problem. It gave the customer the opportunity to be the artist, but getting the tools right on the website proved to be far more difficult than we thought, and it slowed us down getting out of the gate.

While they worked to get the software exactly right, it gave me some time to further assess one of the key stakeholder groups in the Generation Tux operation—our tailors. From the start, they were going to play a huge role in our business. They would be available to run out to a customer's home—or even to the church on the big day—to make on-the-spot alterations in case of a fashion emergency. They would be a critical component to our operation: they would set us apart from my young friends at the Black Tux.

Going back to my days as a kid running around in the Robert Hall stores in the greater tristate area, I'd always been fascinated by and had great respect for these men and women, the unsung heroes of the men's clothing industry. I mean, I loved tailors. Lots of them were immigrants, and lots of them were Jewish—my people. We used to have Tailor Appreciation Day at the Men's Wearhouse. Everybody brought them flowers. We took our tailors out to lunch. It was bigger than Secretaries Day. We treated them like superstars.

In the world of online tux rentals, we were going to make the tailors the human face of the operation. They made up, in real life, the crucial link between the abstract worlds of "high tech" and "high touch," as spelled out in one of my favorite books, *Megatrends: Ten New Directions Transforming Our Lives*, published in 1982 by the author John Naisbitt. The concept was simple: We all loved our apps, our new toys, our newfangled way of doing things. But there had to be the component of soul—some spirit—in the way you manipulated technology, to keep a human element at the forefront of the means of production.

With Generation Tux working out the computer kinks, I decided to start another company that we called zTailors. Again, the idea was simple: You've been working out, and now you're in the best shape of your life. Your clothes are still in pretty good shape, too. The problem is, they no longer fit. Our proposed solution: tap our app or hit us online at our website, and we send the tailor to your house, where he or she does a makeover on the sport coat or suit or whatever that droops over the thirty pounds of space you lost on the Peloton. While they were at it, they might even fix your entire wardrobe.

I liked the way zTailors rolled out. It even had an eco-friendly element, keeping people from throwing away their old clothes. Unfortunately, a few problems that I didn't expect forced us to shut it down prematurely, before we could determine whether the idea held long-term viability.

Problem number one, a lawyer in Los Angeles. He said the tailor we sent out to his house ruined his suit. He demanded $5,000 or—surprise!— he'd sue. We made the business decision to pay him off.

In another case, in New York, one of our tailors filed for unemployment insurance, something that we didn't think you could do if you were hired as an independent contractor, which is the way we set it up on zTailors. We contested the filing, and the case went to an administrative law judge who sided with the tailor. I called the ALJ on the phone to explain to him that the tailor had signed on as an independent contractor, and that I had the paperwork to show him. The ALJ, however, only saw the case from the perspective of the tailor being a hired employee, despite the agreement in which they specifically agreed to be retained as contractors.

I know that some employers in farm labor and construction and the gig economy intentionally misclassify their workers as independent contractors, to screw them out of overtime, lunch breaks, and health benefits. We didn't do that at zTailors. We knew that this was basically after-hours, part-time, on-their-own-time employment, to supplement their incomes. They arranged their appointments with customers around their own schedules. They didn't have to show up in the fields or on construction sites at the break of dawn, or answer to the manipulations of some ride-hailing app.

Despite my sensitivity to labor's arguments in the independent contractor debate, there's just no way we could have made it with zTailors if we had to pay them unemployment between contracts.

From the beginning, the company never made that much money. Now, it had the potential to cost us a lot.

And once again lurking in the darkness: our old pals at the Men's Wearhouse, who saw another way to try and screw us before we got off the ground.

I knew from when I ran the Men's Wearhouse that many tailors, if not most of them, liked to make a few extra bucks working part-time gigs around their full-time jobs. With the zTailors startup, I planned to tap into my network of tailor contacts at my old company to see if they'd like to do some freelancing.

Doug Ewert moved fast to stop it. His high-minded staff put the word out to the company's two thousand tailors—no moonlighting for George. Macy's, okay. Nordstrom—go for it. zTailors—forget about it.

For me, no access to the Men's Wearhouse tailors meant no new company.

It was almost funny. For the third time, the Men's Wearhouse went out of its way to keep me from getting back into the game.

• • •

It took us quite a bit longer than we anticipated to deal with our software problems, but we worked around the trouble in time to blast off in September 2015, at the annual Dreamforce convention—Marc Benioff's San Francisco showcase for the latest in innovation, leadership, new technology, and modern-day mindfulness.

I considered it one of the great honors of my life to share the marquee with the likes of Microsoft CEO Satya Nadella, actress and the Honest Company founder Jessica Alba, Buddhist author Jack Kornfield, San Francisco Giants CEO Larry Baer, and the former Victoria's Secret supermodel turned role model for girl code writers Lyndsey Scott, among many, many others.

In my presentation, I made sure to plug stakeholder capitalism before we highlighted the high-tech, high-touch concept of Generation Tux and how it would change the world of online tuxedo and suit rentals. We finished our presentation with an exquisitely choreographed flash mob of newlyweds and dancers in form-fitted tuxedos that got a rise out of the capacity crowd of several hundred. We parlayed the Dreamforce show to a New Year's Eve celebration in Times Square where I presided over the Generation Tux marriage of a young couple from Miami on one of the most famous streetscapes in the world—and at peak seasonal traffic.

Generation Tux was on the map.

I thought we got a big boost in the interim when we brought in Eric Lane, my favorite COO from the Men's Wearhouse days, to do the same job for Generation Tux. It was so great to have him on my team again, although—depressingly—it was only for a very short three months. He'd barely begun with us before doctors diagnosed Eric with a terminal case of melanoma. He passed away in 2017, and I still miss him.

Eric's absence left me stuck with a shaky cast of executive helpers—my bad, as the one who'd made all the hires. Remembering the eventual lack of cohesion between me and my Men's Wearhouse executives, I saw the signs and wised up in time to give a couple of them the boot before they did too much damage. For one thing, they tried to goof me into a merger where we'd be the underling to a European group that wanted to move in on the online tux-rental business that had been gaining momentum. My (former) people apparently thought it was a good deal. I saw it as an act of sabotage.

Moving on without them, I spent $25 million to acquire a company called Menguin, a new and successful online startup with an inventory of 300,000 garments. I merged their people with our Louisville operation and put them in charge. It wasn't long before we as a combined company were doing a million bucks a month in sales, with projections to more than quintuple our revenues by 2023, with a 40 percent profit margin.

That, of course, was before the coronavirus. For seven weeks in early 2020, we, along with most of the rest of entrepreneurial America, got absolutely killed. Pretty much everybody who ordered a tux for a wedding or a prom canceled on us through the spring. We had to refund a lot of money before we finally flattened our own curve of cancellations. By mid-May, we were getting enough reschedules on cancelled weddings to make me believe that marriage will survive as an American institution. If it proves to be as resilient as I think, we should be fine.

Before the virus hit, we had positioned ourselves beyond the tux. We accommodated the evolving male mindset that had taken a turn against the cluttered closet. Our data show that the clothes hound is dead. Only one out of twenty men these days define themselves as such. Consequently, a good 50 percent of the gender now rent their suits. More and more of them also rent their sport coats. We called ourselves "Generation Tux," but maybe "Generation Suit" would have been more appropriate, or accurate. Suit rentals, we've discovered, make up fully 70 percent of our business.

All of which portends bad news for the small-margin brick-and-mortar retail industry. As somebody who once oversaw an empire of more than 1,100 men's clothing stores, I'd say the chances of the industry surviving as we knew it aren't very good. Most men don't like to go shopping, period. Having to wear a mask, they'll like it even less.

• • •

I still get private equity pitches from some of the most prominent names in that industry, to see whether the Men's Wearhouse is worth a takeover try, and whether I'd be interested in playing a role in what's left of the company.

Nowadays, I take the questions while I sit on the end of my couch in the living room of my home in the Oakland Hills, intermittently puffing on a joint. At age seventy-two, I'm perfectly satisfied to shelter in place—I'd been doing it for years before COVID-19 made its ugly appearance. Hell, I've only got one good eye these days, and the corner of it is usually glued to cable TV news. My two dogs usually lounge close by, if not right next to me on the couch. It's the number-one place where I'd rather be.

I think about the song in *Hamilton* (great musical, by the way) about George Washington's defeat of the redcoats at Yorktown, and the American victory in our Revolutionary War. The change it wrought—the world turned upside down. Coronavirus did that to us again, especially in my old business. Online is going to take up more and more of its future.

I'm more than satisfied and excited about where we're going with Generation Tux. But I still get the private equity inquiries about the Men's Wearhouse, and think about it a little, between puffs. I run some numbers in my brain, and I doodle a little bit on scratch paper, and there's really only one thing I can tell them:

I can't guarantee it.

Epilogue

I never got around to reading Machiavelli until after the board members of the Men's Wearhouse dumped me. Like the millions who read it before and the millions who will read it after me, I seized on the chapter in *The Prince* in which the political consultant to the Renaissance distinguished between a leader motivated by fear and one motivated by love.

"From this arises an argument: whether it is better to be loved than to be feared, or the contrary," Machiavelli wrote more than five hundred years ago. "I reply that one should like to be both one and the other; but since it is difficult to join them together, it is much safer to be feared than to be loved when one of the two must be lacking."

It should really come as no surprise that Machiavelli, in his advice to the ages, came down on the side of fear. We're talking about the guy whose name is now synonymous with "amoral" and "underhanded," used to describe the deceitful and the devious, the self-preserving, the self-dealing, the self-interested corruption that unfortunately motivates so many of the leaders who created our past, control our present, and will decide our future.

St. Francis of Assisi he wasn't.

In the evolution of leadership, the princes who have adhered to Machiavellian counsel have done their best to preserve their power by making damn sure that everybody else is afraid. Not necessarily of the leaders themselves. Just fear of *something*. Of the "other." Of nature and the animals that thrived within it. Of slave revolts. Of abolitionists. Of the working man. Of women's rights. Of unions. Of Jews. Of globalism. Of communism. Of inflation. Of too much democracy.

I would not go so far as to say that the progressive side—my side—has always been lovable, or has been motivated only by love in our search for support. We've stoked our share of fear, too. Maybe Machiavelli had it right. Maybe fear wins out when it is stacked one-on-one against love. Maybe that's just the way of human nature. Maybe Machiavelli had it right about people, that they are "ungrateful, fickle, simulators and deceivers, avoiders of danger, greedy for gain." I don't know about you, but if there is one thing that scares the hell out of me, it's a greedy, fickle simulator with no gratitude who never takes a chance. You run across them everywhere. Even on your own board of directors.

Looking back on my life, there have been many times when I was motivated by fear, mainly a fear of failure. But looking back, I feel I can honestly say that in my own life, in the way I've run my businesses, in the way I've treated my employees, the vendors who supplied my companies, my neighborhoods, my shareholders, and even my competitors, I have acted out of love more than out of fear.

The sixties—they were all about love. We loved those people in Vietnam. We loved the poor, the sick, the impoverished. We loved the earth. I loved the straights as well as the hippies and I loved trying to bring them together. We had a choice between leaders we loved and those we feared. And those whom we chose, we loved.

I loved going on that trip to Asia. I loved doing it for my father, that he loved me so much he introduced me to the one thing he really knew a whole lot about: his industry. In his love for me, he knew that I could make a decent living selling men's clothing, and he loved me enough to let me make my mistakes and let me learn how it worked, in my own way. I loved my mother who always looked out for me, who modeled the virtues of social responsibility, compassion, and generosity, who, against her own instinct, saved me from financial ruin.

I loved Bobby Kennedy more than I feared Nixon, just like I loved Obama more than I feared Trump. I didn't love that guy from Foley's or his canary-yellow sport coats, but I didn't fear him, and I love the fact that I learned so much from the experience—that I came out of it so motivated.

I loved climbing up on that roof with the hand-painted plywood sign that got blown into the parking lot and resulted in the first insurance claim against the Men's Wearhouse. I loved Harry Levy and how he made our computer system sing. I loved Richie Goldman and the passion he brought to marketing us.

I loved building our company into a world leader. I loved the World Business Academy and the Institute of Noetic Sciences and everything I learned about businesses taking care of society as a whole, and how combining science and spirit can propel us toward inquiry, innovation, inner peace, and eternal salvation. I love it that, in California and in other states, we overcame an irrational, misinformed fear of the marijuana plant.

I loved every day of the forty years I spent at the Men's Wearhouse. I loved the seventeen thousand people who worked there when I left, I loved what we accomplished, and I loved the fun I had and the friends I made who will always live deep in my heart.

I loved providing our employees with $10 million in college scholarships through the Zimmer Family Foundation. I loved the kids who benefited, who were in many cases the first in their families to ever attend college. Surprise, Machiavelli. I didn't have to scare any of the four thousand or so employees of the Men's Wearhouse whose families received the scholarships into showing up for work every day. Through the support I offered, the fair wages and benefits that we provided, the fun atmosphere we created in our stores and our shops, and the good times that rolled at our holiday parties, we wanted our people to come to work every day not out of fear for their livelihoods, but out of love for the company.

I've loved getting Generation Tux off the ground, and I love the success I'm sure it will enjoy while I sit here at the end of my couch and watch the A's on television while smoking the best legal cannabis in America.

I think Machiavelli got it wrong. I think a paradigm shift of love over fear is the only way to save America, and the world. I think that leaders need to base everything they do on love—make it the safer bet than fear.

• • •

Tailored Brands filed its bankruptcy papers on a Sunday night, Aug. 2, 2020, a move that became inevitable when the Jos. A. Bank acquisition turned out to be just as bad as I'd expected. It's true that the coronavirus took down some of the biggest names in American retail—JCPenney, Brooks Brothers, and Neiman Marcus, to name a few. And it's true that the growth of online and the demise of brick-and-mortar had been underway for years, even if we'd been able to manage it pretty well at the Men's Wearhouse under my tenure, with our adaptation to the customers' preference for the casual look.

There's no doubt in my mind that the Men's Wearhouse would still be alive and making money and that we would have survived the COVID-19 disaster if I had remained in charge. For one thing, I for sure wouldn't have bought Jos. A. Bank. For another, I wouldn't have fired myself, and people around the world would still know us by the slogan I coined that set us apart—I guarantee it.

In a crisis, it's the calm and steady leader, the trusted figure, who gets you through. I'd done it before, and I'm sure I could have done it again, and it breaks my heart that I didn't get the chance.

"It's a crying shame," I told the *New York Times* reporter when she called me for a quote to go with their story on the Tailored Brands bankruptcy. "I spent forty years creating a really neat company, and it only took seven years to destroy it."

You can also add this to my quote when it comes to the now-failed legacies of Doug Ewert and Bill Sechrest and David Edwab and the rest who acted against me or failed to act on my behalf:

"It couldn't have happened to a nicer bunch of guys."

• • •

Call me an amateur historian, same as you would anybody whose bookshelves are lined with recounts and analysis of how we got to where we are.

Doris Kearns Goodwin, Jon Meacham, and Ron Chernow I'm not, but for what it's worth, here's my take:

For the first two decades of the twentieth century, fear took a back seat in our nation's history. They called it the Progressive Era, and it was mostly a reaction to the Gilded Age, when greed ran America. Under Teddy Roosevelt, and later Woodrow Wilson, the country granted women the right to vote, enacted a progressive income tax, and cracked down on monopolies. States like Wisconsin and California returned power to the people through direct primaries and electoral reforms. The scientific method challenged religion as a way of explaining natural phenomena. We democratized credit. Fact-based, investigative journalism exposed industrial malfeasance and attacked political corruption. Philanthropy marked a new form of benevolent business practice. Conservation programs expanded and the national park system was created. Government stepped in to regulate trade, commerce, food, and drugs. The labor movement grew stronger.

But America's progressive impulse turned out to be fairly short-lived. It died with the onset of World War I and the crackdown on anybody who questioned the US entry into the European conflict. The old Machiavellian fear returned with a vengeance: fear of communist encroachment on American shores, fueled by the successful Bolshevik Revolution in Russia, compounded the conservative reaction.

Then there was President Warren G. Harding. I like to blame him for driving a nail into the progressive coffin and setting the stage for what has mostly been a century of fear. Everybody knows how top officials in the corrupt Harding administration took bribes in the form of federal oil leases in Wyoming and California. But before he presided over the Teapot Dome scandal, Harding, as a US Senator from Ohio, stoked a widespread fear of internationalism that scuttled our entry into the League of Nations. His victory deflected the arc of history just enough to give rise to the Nazi launch of World War II, the Cold War that followed, the rise of Richard Nixon, and the elevation of the McCarthy Era and Roy Cohn. In my view, the arc bends directly to the election of Donald J. Trump, the most successful fearmonger in the history of American politics.

The way I see it, Trumpism rose from the New York real estate market, a hotbed of Machiavellian deceit, of double-dealing, manipulation, trepidation, going back on your word, and, of course, fear. It went national on reality TV, where superficial glamor and drama distracted many viewers from Trump's abject inauthenticity. With his brand burned into the public mind, Trump took on the pose of populist champion, and it appealed to millions of working-class Americans. (Many of the men in that group, I would bet, bought the one and only suit in their closets from the Men's Wearhouse.) They'd been shut out of our country's prosperity, left to struggle on low-paying, dead-end jobs in the widening inequality of our two-tier economy. They'd become susceptible to a message of fear.

The country may have denied Donald Trump a second term as president, but there is no question that, to the great detriment of our national ideals, his politics will remain with us for a long time to come. To me, the rise of Trumpism feels personal, like a repudiation of most of my life. Trumpism, with its race-baiting and nationalism, wants to fight the Vietnam War over again, even though it pleaded "bone spurs" to stay out of the jungle. Trumpism is the guy in Foley's who slit the canary-yellow sport coats and lied to me about making up for it with future business deals. Trumpism is the same thing that made those cops storm off buses outside the fieldhouse at Wash U. and beat the hell out of anti-war protesters. It's like Harry Anslinger's "Reefer Madness" campaign—all fear and no facts.

Trumpism sneers at Siddhartha's journey. It's the opposite of good business practice. It's antithetical to quality, service, and a good price. Trumpism guarantees nothing, except whatever brutality and mendacity is required to ensure its own survival. Trumpism is quintessential shareholder capitalism, with a shareholder of one—Donald Trump, including his immediate family and hangers-on.

Trumpism, in the end, represents the perfection of the rule of fear, the highest manifestation of Machiavellianism.

• • •

Like George Bailey said about money to the angel in *It's a Wonderful Life*, "It comes in real handy down here, bub." And it does. Whether you live in Bedford Falls or Pottersville, you've got to have at least a little bit of it to get through the day.

The question for leaders in government and business, however, is: Are you going to devote your life to chasing money? Or are you, as a leader of a company or a nation—or a sports team, or a foundation, or a rock 'n' roll band—going to go after something more?

I think prioritizing the health and well-being of employees and customers as well as profits is the only way for the capitalist world to sustain itself as the best long-term system to stimulate creativity, prosperity, and freedom. The stakeholder concept is the inoculation against the greed that will destroy the system, from within and without, if the unbridled accumulation of wealth is not checked. Thankfully, the business mindset in our country, and the world, is changing. See for example the most recent statements published out of Davos extolling sustainability. Science tells us that the planet can't sustain itself on a business model where maximizing shareholder value is the only thing that matters. Environmental degradation, in the long run, destroys business as it destroys everything else. Climate change has to be confronted. Big business is beginning to get this. Big business is beginning to pay lip service to the concept of sustainability.

Capitalism rewards entrepreneurship. It celebrates individual initiative. It creates value, and it can be collective. It can spread the wealth and share it with workers, consumers, and the community. It can generate excitement and celebrate the human spirit. To do so, it needs to spread and share the wealth it creates.

Stakeholder capitalism isn't so much about love versus fear. It springs from the intuitive principle that in the search for win-win opportunities, there is none greater than to do unto others what we'd like done to ourselves.

Unconsciously, I operated on the Golden Rule my entire career at the Men's Wearhouse. I was overjoyed when I read John Mackey and Raj Sisodia's book, *Conscious Capitalism*, and saw the outline of the stakeholder concept that provided me with the intellectual description of how I had built my company. Through it all, I valued the people who worked for me, the people who sold to me, the people who bought from me, the people who shared the same airspace as me. I didn't see them as underlings or competitors. They were my partners. They were my brothers and sisters. And when we went public, our shareholders joined the family, too. We took care of them, too—we loved them, too. No more, no less than the sellers, the warehouse workers, the tailors, the vendors, even the regulators. And they loved us back. They showed it in their never-ending, always-growing support, as we shepherded our company through the oil crisis, the dot-com bust, 9/11, the Great Recession, to emerge stronger through each calamity.

My friends in the Occupy movement may not like to hear this, but we loved Wall Street, too, and the feeling was mutual. We did not fear Wall Street or our shareholders, or let them dictate our moral sense. It's probably important to remember, from a political point of view, that half the American people don't own stock in any way, shape, or form, and that most of the people who *do* own it, through their 401ks or their pensions, don't know where it goes or how it works. It's up to business and political leaders, then, to make it work for them.

This is a transition that must occur. That must be sustained. That must spring from the heart and be made to work by the brain. It's a transition that has to be forced by the dominant shareholders, the biggest companies, the high-tech executives whose companies have accumulated some of the greatest levels of wealth the world has ever seen. It is up to them to eliminate fear in their workplace. It is up to them to make their employees happier about their jobs. It is up to them to sacrifice some of their short-term gain for the long-term interest of the planet.

We built the greatest men's clothing company at scale that ever existed. And we did it with love, not fear. We didn't intimidate—we incentivized. The record shows that we created wealth for ourselves and for our shareholders. At the same time, we empowered our workers and our customers, our suppliers and our community. And, almost all the time, we did it without resorting to fear.

Sitting on my couch, in the living room of my home in the Oakland Hills, when I look back at what we did across forty years at the Men's Wearhouse, a baseball metaphor comes to mind.

I took my best swing. I made solid contact. I ran like hell, and as I rounded first base, I saw the ball fly out of the park. I trotted around the bases, and when I finally reached home, I jumped into the air and landed with both feet on the plate, as our customers, our workers, our vendors and even the investors mobbed me.

No matter the Tailored Brands bankruptcy. No matter the treachery of the people I hired and promoted and depended on to take the company into the future but who instead ran it into a ditch.

I went out with a walk-off home run.

Acknowledgments

As we get older, if we're lucky, our memory of our parents gets stronger, as does our gratefulness. My mother passed away thirty-six years ago, and I've only recently come to appreciate her impact on my life and career.

Similarly with my father, who only passed in 2017.

As I acknowledge the army of ghostwriters I've worked with over the ten years this book unfolded, it is, from my perspective, clear who deserves the credit first and foremost: Mom and Dad. How many kids have a twenty-four-year-old orphan for a mom and twenty-five-year-old returning POW as a dad? My desire to survive and succeed is genetic.

In addition to my mother and father, I'd like to acknowledge my four grandparents, all born in New York City, who taught me love, integrity, arithmetic, and responsibility; and my brother and sister, who are both alive and taught me longevity.

My ghostwriters, in order of height, are Kirk Warren, Henry Covey, Marilyn Mandala Schlitz, and Andy Furillo. If you include me at point guard, we average only five feet, eight inches.

My assistant, Allison Smith, is only five foot six inches but is a real slam dunk.

I should also acknowledge my publishers, Richard and Michele Cohn, and their company Beyond Words, a Simon & Schuster imprint. Although we are splitting the proceeds, my share, in its entirety, goes to the Oakland Zoo.

And finally I would like to acknowledge Greg Wilson and Jim Gonzalez who have been part of my marketing and communication strategy for decades.

George Zimmer
Oakland, California
April 2, 2021

I'm to my mother, Marian's, right in this early sixties shot, and then it's clockwise
to my father, Robert, sister Laurie, brother Jimmy, and our dog, Bootsie.

My mother and father on their honeymoon, 1947.

A reflection of my idyllic childhood, with brother Jimmy, sister Laurie—
and Babar the Elephant. Figure about 1955 for this picture.

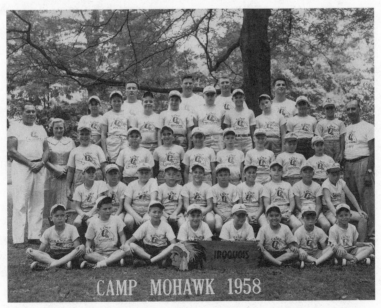

At age 9, I'm the happy camper in the very middle of the first row.

"Papa George" Trosk, my maternal grandfather, about 1940.
Big-time New York lawyer. Taught me the meaning of integrity.

That's my mom and dad in the middle at their Plaza Hotel wedding, January 9, 1947.

I'm holding up sister Laurie and brother Jimmy
in this 1960-ish family shot with my dad, Robert.

I found my tribe at Washington U. with Sigma Alpha Mu, the Jewish fraternity. You can't miss my turtleneck in the middle, and that's my great friend, Harry Levy, at lower left.

Cool in the shades while coming out of college, about 1970.

This was my post-college look that my dad didn't really appreciate.

Rich Goldman and brother Jimmy respectively handled marketing
and merchandising for the CEO (middle).

*1980 – George stands in front of the
Men's Wearhouse Office and Wareh...
facility on Renwick Drive*

The 1980 opening of our first office/warehouse facility merited a big smile.

I didn't goof around in our early commercials like this one from the mid-eighties.

My eyes should tell you I'm pretty drunk in this early eighties picture.
Alcohol and me, we didn't agree.

Dave Stewart gives me some pointers before my opening pitch.
That's Oakland Zoo director Joel Parrott between us.

Throwing out the first pitch in the Oakland Coliseum during the A's late-eighties/
early-nineties heyday. How's my form?

Wardrobe consultant Don Botill hustled up a fit for heavyweight champ Mike Tyson
at one of our Sacramento stores in the late eighties.

In our early years, "Zimmer Bucks" served as an employee incentive.

The first of our "comparison" commercials. The competition hated them.

Demonstrating the proper slo-pitch follow-through at an early company picnic.

Cutting the ribbon on our new Houston office, 1999. That's my lifetime pal Harry
Levy at far right, with my dad, Robert, standing next to him.

Ringing in our listing on the New York Stock Exchange, 2000.
That's me, looking heavenwards, in the middle.

Meet the Zimmer men, 1990 version. That's me on the right, with my dad, Robert, in the middle, and brother Jim on the left.

Three-time UFC heavyweight champion Randy Couture helped us appeal to an edgier clientele.

With my friend Vida Blue, the 1971 American League MVP
and Cy Young Award winner.

I loved Willie so much. I buried him in my yard when it was his time to go.

Pajaro Dunes in the early 2000s was a special place for our family.

Nothing like a baby to bring out a father's joy. My son Kai was one of the last babies
born in the twentieth century at 6:30 PM on January 31, 1999.

With my friend, San Francisco Mayor Willie Brown.

Barack Obama is the future president in this 2008 campaign picture.
I'm giving him some advice on television advertising.

Appendix

Men's Wearhouse Financial Information, 1973–2019

YEAR	SALES	PROFIT*	DEBT	STORES	FT EMP.
1973	$1 million	$0	$1 million	1	10
1983	$5 million	$250,000	$5 million	16	150
1992	$170 million	$11 million	$10.1 million	143	500
1993	$240 million	$15 million	$8.9 million	183	1,000
1994	$317 million	$22 million	$10.8 million	231	2,000
1995	$406 million	$31 million	$24.6 million	278	3,000
1996	$484 million	$38 million	$4.2 million	345	4,900
1997	$631 million	$51 million	$57.5 million	396	6,000
1998	$768 million	$71 million	$57.5 million	431	6,800
1999	$1.19 billion	$101 million	$0	614	10,700
2000	$1.33 billion	$101 million	$46.7 million	651	12,000
2001	$1.27 billion	$73 million	$42.6 million	680	10,800
2002	$1.29 billion	$69 million	$37.7 million	689	11,500
2003	$1.39 billion	$82 million	$38.7 million	693	12,300
2004	$1.55 billion	$118 million	$131 million	707	13,200
2005	$1.72 billion	$165 million	$130 million	719	13,800
2006	$1.88 billion	$149 million	$205 million	752	14,900
2007	$2.11 billion	$147 million	$73 million	784	18,400
2008	$1.97 billion	$58 million	$92.4 million	805	16,200
2009	$1.91 billion	$68 million	$62.9 million	1,259	15,900
2010	$2.10 billion	$101 million	$43.5 million	1,192	16,600
2011	$2.38 billion	$185 million	$0	1,166	17,200
2012	$2.48 billion	$198 million	$0	1,143	17,500
2013	$2.47 billion	$129 million	$0	1,124	18,200
2014	$3.25 billion	$73 million	$97.5 million	1,758	26,100
2015	$3.49 billion	($1.07 billion)	$1.69 billion	1,724	24,500
2016	$3.37 billion	$132 million	$1.66 billion	1,667	22,500
2017	$3.30 billion	$229 million	$1.56 billion	1,477	21,000
2018	$3.23 billion	$212 million	$1.39 billion	1,464	20,600
2019	$2.88 billion	$97 million	$1.16 billion	1,450	19,300

George was fired in 2013. Notice how the numbers trend under the thick black line as opposed to above.

*Earnings Before Interest, Taxes, Depreciation, and Amortization

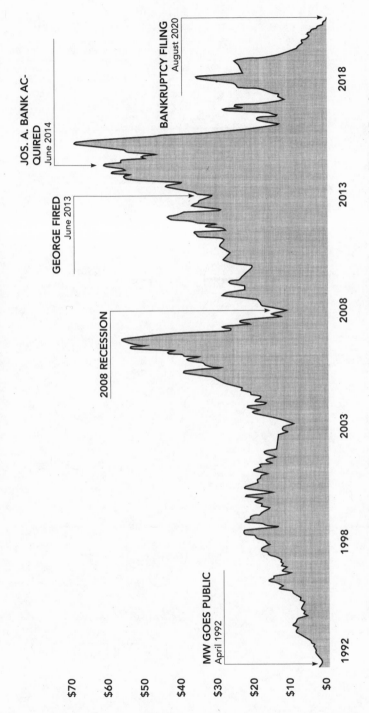

Men's Wearhouse Stock Price, 1992–2020

In January 2016, Men's Wearhouse transitioned to a holding company model under the name Tailored Brands. A short seven years after George's last day, Tailored Brands filed for bankruptcy.

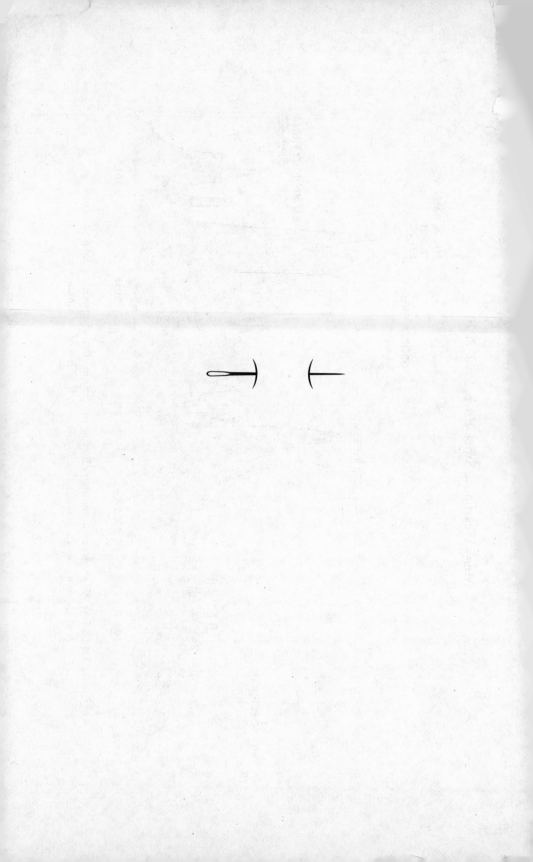